INTERNET STOCK TRADING AND MARKET RESEARCH FOR THE SMALL INVESTOR

INTERNET STOCK TRADING AND MARKET RESEARCH FOR THE SMALL INVESTOR

Paul M. Moubarak

and

Amy E. Steele

iUniverse, Inc.
Bloomington

INTERNET STOCK TRADING AND
MARKET RESEARCH FOR THE SMALL INVESTOR

iUniverse books may be ordered through booksellers or by contacting:

iUniverse
1663 Liberty Drive
Bloomington, IN 47403
www.iuniverse.com
1-800-Authors (1-800-288-4677)

ISBN: 978-1-4759-1360-6 (sc)
ISBN: 978-1-4759-1361-3 (ebk)

Library of Congress Control Number: 2012907000

Printed in the United States of America

iUniverse rev. date: 06/19/2012

To all the individuals who indirectly contributed to this journey . . .

TABLE OF CONTENTS

PREFACE XIII

ACKNOWLEDGMENTS.. XV

INTRODUCTION... XVII

THE ECONOMIC CRISIS OF 2008 xvii
VOLATILITY BENEFITS SHORT-TERM TRADING xviii
THE ADVANTAGE OF SMALL INVESTORS xix
THE INTERNET AND THE ERA OF ONLINE INVESTORS............... xx
WHY IT MATTERS TO BE A TRADER AND A MARKET
ANALYST xxii
BOOK MOTIVATIONS.. xxiii
BOOK ORGANIZATION..xxiv

PART A: STOCK TRADING 1

Chapter 1 MARKET STRUCTURE AND TERMINOLOGIES...... 3
1-1. STOCK EXCHANGE 3
1-2. STOCK INDICES AND AVERAGES.................................... 5
1-3. STOCK SYMBOL.. 8
1-4. MARKET HOURS 9
1-5. STOCK QUOTES AND DATA 10
    1-5-1. **Share Price/Last Trade** 12
    1-5-2. **Share Volume** 12

1-5-3.   **Average Volume** 14

1-5-4.   **Opening and Closing Price** 15

1-5-5.   **52-Week Range** 15

1-5-6.   **Market Capitalization** 17

1-5-7.   **Price Change** 18

1-5-8.   **Ask Price × Ask Size / Bid Price × Bid Size** 18

1-5-9.   **Estimated Metrics of Stock Quotes** 19

1-6.   PRE-MARKET AND AFTER HOUR QUOTES 20

1-7.   STOCK CHARTS 21

1-8.   EARNINGS REPORT 24

1-9.   MISCELLANEOUS DEFINITIONS.....................25

1-9-1.   **Bear Market/ Bull Market** 26

1-9-2.   **Support and Resistance** 26

1-9-3.   **Penny Stock** 27

1-9-4.   **Initial Public Offering (IPO)** 29

1-9-5.   **Stock Split/ Reverse Stock Split** 29

Chapter 2 ONLINE TRADING AND REGULATIONS 31

2-1.   ONLINE BROKERAGE FIRMS.....................31

2-1-1.   **Commission**...32

2-1-2.   **Execution Speed** 33

2-1-3.   **Price Updates** 34

2-1-4.   **Quotes, Charts and Market News** 36

2-1-5.   **Account Maintenance Fee** 37

2-2.   ACCOUNT TYPES 38

2-2-1.   **Cash Account** 38

2-2-2.   **Margin Account**.....................................39

2-3.   ONLINE TRADING TOOLS 40

     2-3-1.   **Trading Long** 40

     2-3-2.   **Trading Short** 41

     2-3-3.   **Buying to Cover** 42

     2-3-4.   **All or None (AON)** 42

     2-3-5.   **Market Order** 43

     2-3-6.   **Limit Order** 44

     2-3-7.   **Stop Order/ Stop Limit Order** 45

     2-3-8.   **Trailing Stop Order/ Trailing Stop Limit Order** 45

2-4.   ONLINE TRADING REGULATIONS 47

     2-4-1.   **Settlement Time/Date** 48

     2-4-2.   **Free Ride** 49

Chapter 3   WEB RESOURCES FOR STOCK TRADING 53

3-1.   ONLINE RESOURCES FOR MARKET DATA 53

3-2.   TOP GAINERS LIST 54

3-3.   TOP LOSERS LIST/ TOP MOST ACTIVE LIST 59

3-4.   OPEN-ACCESS WEB QUOTES 60

3-5.   OPEN-ACCESS INTRADAY AND EXTENDED WEB CHARTS 63

3-6.   EXTENDED-HOURS QUOTES, CHARTS, AND TOP GAINERS LIST 68

3-7.   MARKET NEWS 70

Chapter 4   INTERPRETING MARKET NEWS—PART I 72

4-1.   NEWS WITH MARKET CONNOTATIONS 72

4-2.   ENERGY SECTOR 74

4-3.   PHARMACEUTICAL SECTOR 78

4-4. CONSUMER ELECTRONICS SECTOR 83

4-5. COMMUNICATION SECTOR 86

4-6. OUTTAKE 88

Chapter 5 INTERPRETING MARKET NEWS—PART II 90

5-1. NEWS WITH NO MARKET CONNOTATIONS.................... 90

5-2. EARNINGS REPORT 92

    5-2-1. Exceptional Earnings Reports 92

    5-2-2. Encouraging Earnings Reports 94

    5-2-3. Modest Earnings Reports 95

5-3. MERGER AND ACQUISITION 96

5-4. SECURING A CONTRACT 99

5-5. DELISTING NOTICE 101

5-6. OUTTAKE 102

Chapter 6 CORPORATE NEWS TO AVOID 103

6-1. LIMITED SALE TRANSACTION 104

6-2. CONFERENCE PRESENTATION 105

6-3. EXHIBITIONS 107

6-4. PUBLICATIONS 108

6-5. INITIATION OF MEDICAL STUDIES 110

6-6. APPOINTMENTS 112

6-7. OUTTAKE 113

Chapter 7 RECURRENT INTRADAY PRICE CHART TRENDS 115

7-1. INTRODUCTION 115

7-2. STAIR-LIKE ASCENT 116

7-3. EARLY MORNING SLUMP 117

7-4. SHORT-TERM SELLING TACTICS BASED ON
      SATURATION ZONES 119

7-5. SHORT-TERM SELLING TACTICS BASED ON STRIDE
      LENGTH 122

7-6. ASCENDING STOCKS ON POSITIVE NEWS 124

7-7. DESCENDING STOCKS ON POSITIVE NEWS 125

7-8. OUTAKE 127

PART B: MARKET RESEARCH 129

Chapter 8 OVERVIEW OF TECHNICAL CHART
       ANALYSIS 131

8-1. DEFINITION OF TECHNICAL ANALYSIS 131

8-2. FORMS OF TECHNICAL ANALYSIS 133

    8-2-1. Strong View: Technicians 133

    8-2-2. Semi-Strong View: Random Walkers 133

    8-2-3. Weak View: Fundamentalists 134

8-3. CHARTING STYLES 135

    8-3-1. Candlesticks 135

    8-3-2. Kagi Charts 137

    8-3-3. Renko Charts 138

8-4. CHART PATTERNS 140

    8-4-1. Head and Shoulder Top/Bottom
            Reversal 140

    8-4-2. Double Top/Bottom Reversal 143

    8-4-3. Rising/Falling Wedge 145

    8-4-4. Ascending/Descending Triangles 147

8-5.   MARKET INDICATORS AND OVERLAYS 148

    8-5-1.   **Moving Average**

                  Convergence-Divergence Indicator

                  (MACD).. 150

    8-5-2.   **`Relative Strength Index (RSI)** 151

    8-5-3.   **Bollinger Bands** 153

Chapter 9 SMART SOFTWARE 155

9-1.   WHAT IS SMART? 155

9-2.   MOTIVATIONS OF SMART 155

9-3.   MODES OF OPERATION 157

    9-3-1.   **Best Performers of the Day** 158

    9-3-2.   **Customary Symbols** 159

    9-3-3.   **Timeframes** 159

9-4.   INTERFACE DISPLAYS 160

9-5.   DATA INDEXING 160

9-6.   EXAMPLES 162

9-7.   EXTENDED OPTIONS AND CONCLUSION 163

EPILOGUE 165

RECOMMENDED READINGS 169

GLOSSARY 171

INDEX 179

PREFACE

In today's volatile stock market, technical analysis plays an important role in swinging investors' buying and selling positions. As trading becomes faster and more complicated, mathematical formulas that attempt to model trends in the price chart of a security continue to evolve into a fundamental component of planning trading activities.

With the age of the Internet, stock trading became accessible to a larger selection of investors through online brokerage firms. This made it possible for small investors to participate in the market activities without any financial prerequisites or brokers' assistance.

However, for online investors, trading stocks through a brokerage firm without the assistance of an expert is risky, and may result in significant losses, especially when trading positions are formulated based on speculations, and not on a fundamental understanding of the market dynamics.

This book takes a different approach to Internet stock trading, and simplifies the process of formulating buying and selling positions by tying it to a fundamental analysis of corporate news that drives the market. Its objective is to appeal to the wider selection of online investors and first-time traders who don't necessarily employ technical analysis as a trading compass, as well as to researchers and academics interested in market research and quantitative analysis.

The content of the book is an encompassing introduction to market dynamics and online trading tactics rooted in the authors' unique collaborative business, education, and scientific research perspectives, and is split into two parts. The first part familiarizes the reader with market terminologies and online trade regulations, and presents a discussion on open access web pages that provide free access to market quotes, charts, and corporate news required for the analysis and formulation of trading positions. The investment strategies recommended in this part are based on such free data, and are supplemented by illustrations that visualize factual short-term chart behaviors in response to corporate news and unusual market activity.

The second part presents an introduction to chart trends and common technical indicators and overlays. However, the main objective is to discuss the capabilities of a special-purpose experimental financial tool called *SMART* (an acronym for Stock-data for Market Analysis and Research Tools).

SMART's interface is developed by the authors in compliance with free market data that public companies share on open-access web pages. Its purpose is to enable individual market researchers to retrieve intraday price and volume data required for testing the feasibility of any prospective market models.

Such data is normally sold for a price tag that is largely unaffordable by independent researchers. The aim of SMART is to broaden the access to this data in order to encompass any individual with interest in market research, and to eliminate the prerequisite of financial database subscriptions which represent a fundamental component of such research activities.

The strategies, recommendations, and trading materials presented in this book represent the synthesis of three years of daily market research and analysis, and are a derivative of the important lessons learned from online active trading over the same period.

ACKNOWLEDGMENTS

The authors wish to acknowledge Rita Moubarak for her contribution to the design of the book cover, Jack Moubarak for editing the online tutorials in support of the software presented in the last chapter of the book, and Danielle Barsky for narrating the tutorials.

INTRODUCTION

THE ECONOMIC CRISIS OF 2008

On September 15th 2008, Lehman Brothers, once the oldest and fourth largest investment bank in the United States, filed for Chapter 11 bankruptcy protection. The filing, regarded as the greatest bankruptcy in American history, triggered a massive destruction in asset values in the wake of the panic that followed, causing the Dow Jones Industrial index to lose more than five thousand points in the five months that followed the filing.

To many analysts, the bankruptcy of Lehman Brothers was considered as the seminal event that prompted the global recession, which was further amplified by the subsequent panic reaction and the loss of confidence in the market. This loss of confidence transpired into a high level of lingering volatility that continues to impact the global markets, as the foundations of the economy remain vulnerable to the unsettled consequences of the fiscal and monetary policies that sustained the crisis in the first place.

In this environment of financial uncertainty, shareholders saw their equity value disintegrate as investors exited the market. Even as a temporary recovery was instigated in the two years following the crisis, the root-cause of the financial problem was never acknowledged. This meant that the effective solutions that would have otherwise rebalanced the market and created a new equilibrium point from which real growth can be seen were distorted through monetary intervention.

This intervention inhibited the real consequences of the crisis from unfolding, but in the process, exacerbated the problem by sustaining a more enduring period of financial instability. The consequences of this long-term instability will likely not be lessened unless the market is allowed to auto-correct itself by purging the risky investments that caused the collapse. Until that happens, the stock market will remain over-priced, and the high volatility rate will continue to shape its direction on an intraday basis.

VOLATILITY BENEFITS SHORT-TERM TRADING

In this environment of uncertainty, the traditional dynamics of the market where investors hold stakes in public companies to take advantage of appreciation over an extended period of time will not function properly. The over-valuation of stocks in fact makes them more susceptible to losing value as they reach a saturation level in a climate where the market is sustained by stimulated economic growth.

Until a price equilibrium point is established through depreciation, the best outlet for deriving profit on the stock market remains through short-term trading. This form of trading takes advantage of investment opportunities whenever they present themselves, and exits the market when the upward momentum slows down, either during the same intraday session or shortly thereafter.

While this strategy does not raise capital for public companies and does not entitle investors to any dividends, it provides liquidity for the market whilst shielding investors from the drawbacks of extended volatility. In this process, trading positions are formulated based on the interpretation of corporate news for connotations that create a high positive volatility on the stock, thus enabling it to gain significant value on short-term basis. This type of corporate news is normally released on a frequent basis, which raises the likelihood of short-term profit that could far exceed the cumulative profit generated from traditional long positions based on stock appreciation.

THE ADVANTAGE OF SMALL INVESTORS

Investors with *modest* portfolios are most adequately positioned to take advantage of traditional market trends, as well as positive market volatility in a climate of global economic uncertainty. These small investors—as they are commonly known—possess the portfolio that enables them to buy and sell stocks into virtually any public corporation without being dictated by the company's minimum market capitalization and average daily volume. This is in contrast to large investors whose trading options are dictated by such considerations, and whose investments are limited to big corporations that trade on heavy daily volumes with high market capitalizations.

By being free of these market considerations, small investors can maximize their profit by taking advantage of short-term positive trends that characterize the movement of small-cap stocks on relatively low volumes. Such stocks can generate triple digit profit during a single trading session marked by a major news release, even in a period of bear markets where larger investors are uncertain about the direction of the global economy and its impact on their investments.

From a trading perspective, the difference between large and small investors lies in the influence that the latter exhibits on the short-term momentum of a stock. This influence is relatively minimal in comparison to the overall trend that defines this momentum during trading sessions marked by major news releases.

As a result, a small investor acquiring a stake in a stock at the beginning of a trading session and selling it shortly thereafter, causes minimal swings in the share price during the execution of the buying and selling orders. Such dynamics enable small investors to ride the upward wave of positive volatility created by the unusual volume in reaction to a major news release, and exit the market without impacting the stock price or the profit they derive from such temporary trends.

Those dynamics do not act in favor of larger investors whose investment ability results in significant swings in the stock price of small corporations. If these investors were to acquire a large stake in a small-cap company during a session of unusual volume (driven by a major news release), this investment would induce a clear impact on the stock chart where it causes a substantial swing in the intraday share price.

Such behavior is evidenced by an instant spike in the price when the buying order is executed, counteracted by an instant dip that offsets the price hike when the selling order is complete. These price swings deter large investors from either trading, or placing large orders on small-cap stocks even when they are marked by a major press release.

In contrast, small investors can derive a significant profit from the reaction of the market to positive news reports, by taking advantage of volatility and the subsequent unusual volume without being affected by the substantial swings that large investors create on the stock.

THE INTERNET AND THE ERA OF ONLINE INVESTORS

The advent of the Internet revolutionized the dynamics of stock trading and enabled more investors to be involved in the market activities than ever before. This technology dramatically increased the interest of small individual investors in the stock market, as the prospects of deriving profit and managing investment portfolios were made possible from the comfort of their personal computer.

As a result of the Internet, online brokerage firms were created to act as a hub between online investors and the market. These firms reshaped the modality of stock trading, which in the past, relied solely on stock brokers to link investors to market activities by receiving investment orders over the telephone and executing them on the trading floors.

In this Internet era, traditional brokers are replaced by trading platforms that enable investors to manage their positions and place orders directly online through an automated system. This system streamlines the process of stock trading and reduces the order execution time to a few seconds, which enables investors to react to fast moving market trends and benefit from positive volatility.

Online trading platforms also provide investors with the tools to research the market and analyze stock quotes, news, and charts before formulating their trading positions. These tools are further supplemented by open access web pages, which provide real-time free access to market data in the form of extended charts, quotes, and press releases for all publicly traded companies.

This combination of online brokerage firms and open-access market data made stock trading easier and more convenient than ever before. As a result, more investors—especially those with moderate portfolios—are encouraged to participate in the market activities to draw profit on capital investments or build their retirement funds.

This web-driven trading trend is projected to strengthen, as more individuals realize the short-term benefits of the stock market and take advantage of the online technology to participate in the trading activities.

WHY IT MATTERS TO BE A TRADER AND A MARKET ANALYST

Trading stocks is an inherently risky process in which novice investors can inflict considerable loses to their accounts if they formulate their trading positions based on speculations. This process can be even riskier for online investors who often originate their orders without the assistance of a market expert.

However, it is important to note that even the best market experts are prone to mistakes, and that even the most reliable financial models exhibit limited consistency with respect to their ability to predict the direction of the market. These predictive efforts become predominantly more arduous and less accurate when the market is dominated by uncertainty in a lingering climate of economic slowdown, which further lessens the likelihood of profit.

In such environment, the safest strategy for minimizing risk exposure is to trade on a short-term strategy, based on an interpretation of corporate news and extended charts for positive market connotations. Because such connotations cannot be modeled statistically as they depend on the content of press releases, the only outlet to deriving profit from the unusual market reaction when such news is released is through an educated interpretation of these implicit connotations on daily basis.

This interpretation enables the formulation of sound trading positions based on factual analyses rather than speculations, but requires investors to understand the market dynamics in order to lessen the risk of loses. This means that, in order to maximize the likelihood of profit from short-term trading positions, individual investors have to acquire the knowledge of online investing, in addition to the skills of market analyses and corporate news interpretation.

The time invested in learning to analyze corporate news is worthwhile, nonetheless. This is because news reports represent the forces that shape the market's direction, and learning how to interpret them gives investors a well-founded tool to derive profit from the market under normal conditions, as well as during periods of economic uncertainty.

Furthermore, the advantage of using market connotations as a trading compass instead of technical indicators appeals to a broader pool of investors who favor non-technical methodologies to analyze the market. This makes stock trading more accessibly profitable to such investors, while concurrently supplementing the trading strategies of technical investors.

BOOK MOTIVATIONS

The objective of this book is to appeal to the broad readership of online investors with interest in stock market activities on a short-term basis. The content of this book brings a unique insight into market analysis from a perspective of corporate news interpretation and extended chart analyses. Unlike traditional literature where recommended trading strategies are mainly formulated based on technical and statistical indicators; this book simplifies the dynamics of stock trading by tying the market analysis to a direct interpretation of the connotations exhibited in corporate news.

The significance of this strategy is two-folded. On one hand, the analysis of the stock market based on news connotations requires no prerequisites or database subscriptions that provide access to technical chart information. Instead, news interpretation is solely accomplished using free public market data available on open-access web pages, which further broadens the appeal of this recommended approach.

On the other hand, using corporate news as a market compass for formulating trading positions represents a safe investment strategy which is largely unaffected by the overall economic climate. This enables technical and non-technical investors to profit from news-driven trends on a short-term basis, while lessening the risk of loss exposure by benefiting from the recurrent aspects of such trends.

BOOK ORGANIZATION

The content of this book is organized in two parts, with the objective of appealing to non-technical online investors seeking capital profit on short-term investments, and to technical investors and academics interested in market research and quantitative analysis.

PART A introduces investors to the dynamics of online stock trading from all relevant perspectives. This includes a familiarization with market terminologies and online trade regulations, as well as with open access web pages that provide instant free access to market quotes, charts, and news on a daily basis.

The trading strategies recommended in *Part A* are based on such open access data. These strategies are mainly focused on cheap stocks (under $10), and are derived from the interpretation of corporate news for market connotations that generate a significant increase in the stock price on short-term basis. Such analysis is supplemented by an interpretation of extended price and volume charts in order to strengthen the soundness of trading positions.

Part A also presents a discussion on the most recurrent chart trends that online investors are encouraged to adopt in order to time their short-term buying and selling positions. This discussion is extended to include an analysis of chart trends and corporate news that do not create a positive momentum, and which should be avoided by investors when formulating trading positions.

All these recommendations represent the synthesis of three years of daily market research and analysis, and are supplemented by graphical illustrations that visualize factual chart behaviors in response to corporate news and unusual short-term activity on the stock market.

PART B is tailored more towards investors, economists and academics with interests in market research and quantitative statistics used to model the behavior of the market, or the performance of a specific stock on short-term and long-term bases.

The content of this part is therefore research-oriented. Its main objective is to provide interested individuals with a tool that enables access to free discrete-time stock data at the end of every trading session. This data—which is normally sold as monthly or quarterly subscriptions for a price tag that is largely unaffordable by small investors—allows interested market researchers to develop their own intraday discrete-time databases for any selected stocks trading on the floors of NYSE, NASDAQ, and AMEX.

Stock-data saved in this database is compatible with any off-the-shelf financial or statistical tool (such as MATLAB, SAS, Excel), which can be used to develop, test and validate the statistical effectiveness of prospective market models.

The content of *Part B* is therefore structured around a special-purpose experimental software interface dubbed **SMART**, an acronym for *Stock-data for Market Analysis and Research Tools*. SMART's interface is built in compliance with free stock data that public companies share on open-access web pages. This includes discrete time history of price change and corresponding share volume over the course of every trading session.

Market data retrieved through SMART's computational engine is saved in a spreadsheet format inside databases that SMART creates and indexes automatically on the host computer. *Part B* therefore presents an introduction to the fundamentals of technical analysis, and discusses the capabilities of SMART and its different features and operation modes along with relevant case studies and illustrative examples. This discussion on SMART is further supported by narrated web tutorials available on *YouTube* Channel: www.youtube.com/user/ STOCKTRADINGBOOK.

Altogether, *Part A* and *Part B* intend to provide online investors with a full and complete introduction to the stock market activities from the perspective of online stock trading and corporate news analysis. Henceforth, it is the object of this book to appeal to the ever-growing trend of technical and non-technical online stock investors, by providing trading strategies that minimize risk exposure and maximize capital profit on short-term investments.

PART A

STOCK TRADING

Chapter 1

MARKET STRUCTURE AND TERMINOLOGIES

1-1. STOCK EXCHANGE

A stock exchange represents the floor on which most trading and brokerage activities take place, and constitutes the entity that regulates and controls the exchange and pricing of equities between buyers and sellers. In the United States, there are three major trading floors located in the financial district of New York City.

These floors are known as the New York Stock Exchange (NYSE), the National Association of Securities Dealers Automated Quotations (NASDAQ), and the American Stock Exchange (AMEX), the latter representing an integral body of NYSE. Together, these three stock exchange entities encompass a total listing of 5,189 public American and International companies (as of 2011).

All three exchange floors share a reasonable amount of similarities and have to adhere to the regulations imposed by the federal regulatory commission (known as Securities and Exchange Commission or SEC) of the United States. However, their modes of operation differ in many aspects, most notably with respect to listing/delisting requirements and maintenance fees. For instance, companies listed on NYSE are required to maintain a minimum market capitalization of $50 million, while the minimum market capitalization for listing requirements on NASDAQ is $1.1 million.

Maintenance fees also largely differ between stock exchanges, where NYSE imposes more expensive and stringent listing fees in comparison to NASDAQ. As such, companies listed on NYSE normally represent an agglomeration of the largest most prestigious and least volatile public corporations in America, which possess high market capitalization and can afford listing fees. NASDAQ exchange body on the other hand agglomerates smaller corporations, including those with share pricing under $1, and those companies with low trading volumes and higher price volatility.

In the event where a company trading on the floors of any of the regulated stock exchanges fails to comply with the listing requirements—such as in the event of bankruptcy or failure to maintain a share price above $1 for an extended duration of time—it normally becomes delisted to one of the Over-The-Counter markets better known as OTC or Pink Sheets.

These markets are not subjected to the same regulations that govern the organized stock exchanges, and encompass delisted corporations and firms with a very small market capitalization and a small number of shareholders (as low as 300 shareholders in some cases). As a consequence, OTC and Pink Sheet stocks are very risky and extremely volatile.

From an investment perspective, it is important to understand that the stock exchange under which a company trades is of little relevance to investment decisions, in particular when the objective is short-term buying and selling activities. For individual investors, the most important aspect about stock exchanges and the difference between the organized bodies of NYSE, NASDAQ and AMEX is the share price, the short-term return prospects and the volatility rate of a specific stock.

Companies trading on NYSE are in general more stable with expensive share pricing (above $10) and low prospects for high short-term returns. In comparison, companies listed under NASDAQ and AMEX

4

are less expensive (under $10) and subsequently more volatile, but often possess the ability to generate large single-day gains and short-term returns under low trading volumes.

Moreover, for online trading activities, only public companies with stocks listed under NYSE, NASDAQ and AMEX can be traded electronically through an online brokerage firm. In principle, an individual investor placing orders online should be capable of buying and selling stocks of any listed public company. However, it is not uncommon that brokerage firms impose buying restrictions on some cheap stocks, especially those with high volatility rates and low average daily trading volumes. OTC and Pink Sheet stocks on the other hand cannot be traded through online brokers and are not accessible to such investors.

1-2.   STOCK INDICES AND AVERAGES

Stock indices and averages represent a statistical metric that measures the performance of the market as a whole, or the performance of specific sectors of the market on daily basis and over the course of a period of time. These indices reflect the general *mood* and direction of the market, and are used as indicators of the growth or decline of local and global economies.

From a statistical perspective, stock indices normally encompass a listing of stocks that share common market characteristics. Some indices agglomerate stocks attributed to the same industry or commodity, such as an agglomeration of technology or mining companies. Others encompass corporations that share similar trading characteristics, such as similar capitalizations or similar daily trading volumes.

The methodologies used to calculate the value of the average also differ from one index to the other. For instance, the Dow Jones

Industrial Average (DJIA) (Figure 1.1) which encompasses thirty large public corporations in the United States, calculates the value of the index based on the price change of the stock during the trading session, without any consideration for the stock volume or market capitalization. Other indices, such as the S&P 500 and the NYSE and NASDAQ Composite (Figure 1.1) are more encompassing, and use capitalization-weighted compensators to account for the difference in companies' market size and trading activities.

Typically, market analysts, economists, and journalists rely on stock indices to interpret the behavior of the market and indicate the health of the local and global economy. In the United States for example, there are many such indices, with the most popular being the Dow Jones, the NASDAQ Composite and the NYSE Composite.

These three indices encompass a large body of American public companies and serve as an indicator for the overall health of the local economy. An illustration of the relevance of these indices is shown in Figure 1.1, where a sample five-year history of the three leading American indices is plotted between 2006 and 2011.

In this figure, it is obvious that a decline in the indices coincides with a period of economic instability such as the financial collapse of Wall Street experienced between 2008 and 2009. On the other hand, a market growth period similar to the one exhibited prior to, and after the financial collapse of 2008 is accompanied by a positive trend in the indices.

To individual investors, despite the relevance of statistical indices and their usefulness as overall market indicators, these averages should only be regarded as abstract measures of the overall market direction, and should not be used to formulate buying and selling positions related to a specific stock. This recommendation can be made more sensible if one realizes that stock indices are statistical methodologies whose values are largely influenced by the movement of larger corporations that normally drive the market.

Figure 1.1. Chart showing the behavior of the Dow Jones, the NASDAQ Composite, and the NYSE Composite over a period of five years (from 2006 to 2011). Note the collapse in the averages between 2008 and 2009 as a result of the economic recession (*Source:* finance.yahoo.com)

This means that the individual movement of companies with small market capitalization and low trading volumes is often overshadowed by big market drivers, since the formers' influence on the market direction is minimal. Therefore, it is important to realize that a negative movement in a stock index does not necessarily translate into a similar movement for all companies encompassed by the index. In fact, it is not an uncommon occurrence on the market that stocks of smaller companies be spiking during trading sessions dominated by negative trends in major indices, and that conversely, stocks of large corporations be losing value during trading sessions with positive trends in the indices.

1-3. STOCK SYMBOL

A stock symbol or ticker symbol is a combination of one, two, three, or four letters (rarely numbers) that uniquely abbreviate the name of a public company trading on a stock exchange floor. These symbols are also used to associate news, quotes, technical analysis and trading activities with the corresponding stocks of the public firm.

One-, two-, and three-character symbols are normally reserved for the stocks of NYSE, while AMEX stocks are generally denoted by three characters, and NASDAQ stocks by four. Examples of these different categories of symbols are provided in Table 1.1.

Table 1.1. A list of sample stock symbols of different character length with corresponding company name and market

Stock Symbol	Company Full Name	Stock Exchange
C	Citigroup, Inc.	NYSE
KO	The Coca Cola Company	NYSE
BAC	Bank of America Corporation	NYSE
SLV	iShares Silver Trust	AMEX
LEE	Lee Enterprises, Incorporated C	AMEX
YHOO	Yahoo! Inc.	NASDAQ
EBAY	eBay Inc.	NASDAQ

In some cases, stock symbols may include more than four letters, and may even include other special characters such as hyphens (-) and periods (.). A fifth letter appended to a NASDAQ stock symbol, or a series of letters appended to the original NYSE or AMEX symbol through hyphens or periods, indicate that there are special considerations about the stocks of the corresponding firm.

For instance, a company's symbol hyphenated with the letter *A* or *B* indicates the specific class of the stock. For example, *Berkshire Hathaway* stocks with symbol *BRK* are divided into two categories; *BRK-A* denoting the class *A* of the stock (the more expensive stock), and *BRK-B* denoting the class *B* of the stock (the less expensive stock). On the other hand, suffixes *.PK* and *.OB* appended to the end of the stock symbol refer to pink sheets and over-the-counter trading, respectively.

Online trading orders can only be executed using the appropriate stock symbol. Therefore, it is important for investors to familiarize themselves with these abbreviations and the connotations they may carry, such as the market where a specific stock is traded, which is often reflected by the character length of the symbol. Stocks with special characters in the abbreviation ("-" and ".") are normally not available for trading through online brokerage firms. Data and quotes for these stocks may also be rarely available on open-access web pages and online resources.

1-4. MARKET HOURS

In the United States, trading hours are divided into three sessions: Early trading hours, Regular market hours and After-hours.

The early trading session, or pre-market hours, starts at 4:30 AM (EST) in the morning and ends at the opening of the regular trading session at 9:30 AM (EST). The regular market hours start at 9:30 AM, right after the closing of the pre-market hours, and end at 4:00 PM (EST), while the after-hours start at 4:00 PM and end at 8:00 PM (EST) in the evening. Exceptions are some holidays, where extended (pre-market and after-hours) and regular trading hours are shortened, most notably the regular hours which end at 1:00 PM (EST) instead of 4:00 PM (EST).

The objective of the extended trading hours is to allow investors to react to news reports released prior to the beginning, or after the closing of the regular trading session. Although this may generally be profitable during the early trading hours where the trading volume and optimism are normally higher; it is rather less profitable in the after-hours where the volume is lower and the price is more volatile. In any case, the bulk of the trading activities will always occur during the regular hours as these are longer and available to a larger body of investors.

For individual investors, it is safer to trade during regular market hours, as these follow very strict operating schedules and attract significantly larger volume activities. Online trading is in most cases available for small investors only during regular hours, since pre-market and after-hour sessions are normally reserved to privileged and institutional investors. For this reason, individual investors are encouraged to trade during regular hours to avoid the irregularities of extended sessions which may be unavailable, interrupted, delayed, or even terminated abruptly without any prior notice depending upon the volume activity of the stock.

1-5. STOCK QUOTES AND DATA

Stock quotes represent a list of metrics that characterize the movement of a stock during regular market hours, and summarize relevant statistical measures about the stock performance over the course of a period of time.

Unlike intraday quotes which reflect the performance of a stock during regular market hours (9:30 AM to 4:00 PM), pre-market and after-hour quotes have a lesser importance, especially to online investors who typically have no access to these trading activities. As such, this section focuses on intraday quotes, and reserves the discussion on pre-market and after-hours quotes to section 1-6.

Understanding and correctly interpreting intraday quotes is a critical aspect of stock trading, as the information they carry directly influences the performance of a stock during every instance of the trading session. Depending upon the source of information, updates for intraday stock quotes can be available to online traders either instantaneously, or can be delayed by 15 to 20 minutes.

A sample stock quote depicted in Figure 1.2 shows a summary of the metrics that are normally calculated during intraday trading sessions. Although some quotes are more detailed than others (depending upon the source), quote metrics in general exhibit different levels of importance, where some metrics forge a higher impact on the stock performance than others. Therefore, in the following paragraphs, the focus will be on discussing those metrics that play a major role in framing trading decisions during regular market hours.

Bank of America Corporation Com (NYSE: BAC)

REAL-TIME 11.48 ↑ 0.02 (0.13%) 9:59AM EDT

Last Trade:	11.51	Day's Range:	11.35-11.58
Trade Time:	9:44AM EDT	52wk Range:	10.91-16.20
Change:	↑ 0.05 (0.44%)	Volume:	11,775,392
Prev. Close:	11.46	Avg Vol (3m):	133,053,000
Open:	11.35	Market Cap	116.63B
Bid:	11.52 x 47600	P/E (ttm):	N/A
Ask:	11.53 x 42700	EPS (ttm):	-0.47
1y Target Est:	17.38	Div & Yield:	0.40 (0.40%)

Figure 1.2. A sample online stock quote for Bank of America (BAC)
(*Source:* finance.yahoo.com)

1-5-1. Share Price/Last Trade

One of the most important metrics quoted for a stock in real-time is the share price and its variations over the course of a trading session. A share price denotes the amount of money a buyer is expected to pay in order to acquire a single share in the company's common stock offering. Access to this information is therefore critical, as it depicts the number of shares an investor can buy with a given monetary investment.

Variations in the share price during every trading session is dictated by a number of factors, most notably, by the volume of buying orders compared to the volume of selling orders obeying the laws of supply and demand.

Share price increases when the buying volume exceeds the selling volume. This, for instance, occurs when a company releases positive news that enthuses investors to purchase stakes in the company's stock offering, thus driving the share price up. On the other hand, a share price loses value when the selling volume outweighs the buying volume, such as in the aftermath of a news release depicting a disappointing company's performance. A share price will maintain the same price if no buying or selling interests are exhibited in the stock.

1-5-2. Share Volume

Share volume represents another important metric quoted for a stock in real-time. The share volume, or volume for short, represents the sum of the total number of shares bought or sold during a given period of time, or over the course of one trading session.

Share volume can be regarded as a measure of daily activity and interest in a specific stock. A buying or selling order placed during high volume trades can be executed almost instantaneously, at or near the desired price. In contrast, orders placed at low volume activities may require an extended amount of time to be executed, and may even only be processed at an undesirable price dictated by the availability of buyers and sellers.

Stock volume therefore reveals the amount of liquidity in a stock. In the simplest form possible, liquidity can be defined as the ease of buying into a stock, and the ease of selling or getting out of a stock. If a stock is trading at low volume, the number of investors buying and selling into the stock is low, which typically results in large price fluctuations between one order and the other.

A sample example shown in Figure 1.3 illustrates an intraday price chart for a stock trading at low volume (6,000 shares for the whole trading session). In this chart, a selling order of 2,900 shares placed during the first 30 minutes of the session caused the stock to drop in value by 21% (from $3.5 to $2.75). Subsequently, buying orders totaling 2,100 shares placed during the remainder of the session caused the stock to gain 26% in value.

These high price fluctuations are typical of stocks trading at low volume, which means that a large market selling order placed at low volume may likely be executed at a much lower price than the desired one. By the same token, a large market buying order placed at low volume may be executed at a price much higher than the desired one.

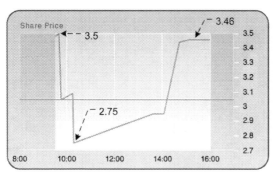

Figure 1.3. A stock trading at low volume (6,000 shares) with high volatility (*Source:* www.nasdaq.com)

13

Typically, there exist no thresholds as to what constitutes a low trading volume and what constitutes a high trading volume. This is mainly because the trading volume is a time-dependant metric that changes over the course of the trading session, while being influenced by many other market factors such as the share price.

As a rule of thumb for Internet investors, stocks trading under 100,000 shares per day can be considered as low volume securities associated with high price fluctuations and low liquidity. On the other hand, stocks trading with a daily volume above 100,000 shares can offer better prospects for higher liquidity.

1-5-3.   Average Volume

The average volume is a statistical indication of the daily trading volume of a specific stock. This is normally calculated as the total intraday share volume averaged over a period of three months or a full year (depending upon the source), as opposed to the daily share volume which is calculated over the course of every individual intraday session.

Typically, the average volume is regarded as a rough general indicator of the level of activity and interest in the stock. Under normal trading sessions unmarked by a major news release, a stock will likely trade near the average volume over the course of the intraday session. In this case, the average volume will be useful for investors to assess the level of liquidity in the stock, and remain cautious about placing large buying orders with stocks characterized by low average volumes.

However, in the event where a stock is marked by an important current or prospective corporate action such as the release of an earnings report, the interest in the stock will very likely increase, and the daily share volume will exceed the average volume by a noticeable amount. This is known as an unusual trading volume, and sessions marked by such market events imply that the average volume has no market significance since the stock is behaving in an unusual fashion.

In this case, investors should discard any connotations the average volume may exhibit with respect to liquidity and price fluctuation, and make trading decisions based on the significance of the corporate news as will be discussed later in Chapters 4, 5 and 6.

1-5-4.   Opening and Closing Price

The opening price denotes the price at which the stock started the trading session at 9:30 AM (EST). The opening price does not account for the share price during the pre-market hours preceding the market opening at 9:30 AM.

The closing price denotes the price of the stock during the last trade before the closing of the market at 4:00 PM (EST). This metric too does not account for the price that the stock achieves during the extended after-hour session.

1-5-5.   52-Week Range

The 52-Week range depicts the highest and lowest price the stock has reached in the past year of trading. This range is not calculated based on the highest and lowest opening and closing prices that the stock achieved in the past year. Instead, the 52-Week range is calculated based on the highest and lowest price the stock has attained during any regular trading session in the previous year, irrespective of the opening and closing price.

For example, consider a stock with a 52-Week range of $1-$2.2 trading during a regular session with an opening price of $2.1. If the stock reaches a peak value of $2.5 at 1:00 PM and closes the session at a price of $2.3, then the 52-Week range will be updated to $1-$2.5 and not to $1-$2.3. This fact is important to understand in order to avoid confusion when analyzing an extended price chart (discussed in section 1-7) which only records the opening and closing price of the stock during every intraday session. Therefore, it should not be surprising to note a price difference between the upper bound of the 52-Week range, and the highest value shown on the stock's price chart for the same period of time (1 year).

Although not largely deterministic, the 52-Week range represents an important metric that reflects the level of overpricing, or otherwise undervaluation of the stock price. A stock is dubbed undervalued when its current price falls within the close proximity of the lower bound of the 52-Week range. This means that, under an encouraging performance of the company, the stock will likely regain value without a major fear of price overvaluation.

This level of overpricing is determined by the difference between the share price and the upper bound of the 52-Week range. In the case of undervaluation, the difference is normally large. Thus, a stock price hovering around the lower bound will possess considerable potential to increase in value, provided that it is sustained by optimism and a positive outlook about the company's performance.

On the other hand, a stock starts to become overpriced when its value is pushed closer towards the upper bound of the 52-Week range. At the upper bound, it becomes more likely that the stock loses value, especially if the positive increase in the stock price is not supported by strong news and a solid market outlook for the company.

Nevertheless, a stock trading at the vicinity of the upper bound can always establish a new high when sustained by optimism, which normally results from the release of positive news with long-term market connotations. Such news can drive the stock into new territories, and the stock's 52-Week range will be updated accordingly to reflect this positive momentum.

1-5-6. Market Capitalization

The market capitalization, or market cap for short, determines the monetary value of a company's total public assets, and is calculated by multiplying the share price of the company's public stock offering by the number of issued shares. A company's size is therefore determined by its market cap, and public firms are ranked, based on this information, into large corporations, mid-cap corporations and small corporations.

From a trading perspective, the market cap is most useful in evaluating the significance of a news release containing explicit monetary information, such as the awarding of new contracts and their values. For example, for a company whose market cap is $10 million, an awarded contract worth $5 million represents 50% of the company's public asset value. This will generate a significant interest in the company's stock, which could cause the share price to rise considerably during the trading session following the news release.

Small-cap companies marked by such news release can be an invaluable opportunity for investors interested in high returns on short-term investments. On the other hand, the same news released by a company with a market cap of $100 million will likely have a minimal impact on investors' interest in the stock, and will subsequently not generate a comparable rise in the share price.

1-5-7. Price Change

The price change represents a comparison between the price of a share during any given trading session, and the closing price of the previous session. This is normally referred to as the daily price change, and is calculated by subtracting the current price from the previous closing price, and dividing the difference by the previous closing price to express the change as a weighted percentage

$$Daily\ Price\ Change\ (\%) = \frac{Current\ Price - Previous\ Closing\ Price}{Previous\ closing\ price}$$

The daily percent change is influenced by many market factors such as a news release. Positive news normally tends to drive the share price up, while negative news tends to drive the share price down, along with the price percent change. To distinguish one behavior from the other, the daily price change is color-coded, where a green-colored price change signals an increase in the share value, and a red-colored price change signals a decrease in the share value relative to the previous closing price.

1-5-8. Ask Price × Ask Size / Bid Price × Bid Size

In the context of stock trading, the ask price or sell price denotes the minimum price a seller of a stock is willing to accept for selling a share of that stock. The size of this transaction, or the number of shares the seller is willing to sell at the ask price, is called the ask size. These two metrics are normally bundled together into a single expression with the "×" character separating the ask price from the ask size. For example, an order of 2.15×2,000 means that a seller is willing to sell 2,000 shares of the stock at a price of $2.15/share.

The bid price, or buying price, denotes the maximum price a buyer of a stock is willing to pay in order to buy a share of that stock. Similar to the ask price, the bid price is always associated with a bid size which denotes the number of shares a buyer is willing to purchase at the bid price. Bid price and bid size are also bundled together into an expression separated by the character "×", such as 1.12×1,000, which denotes a buying order of 1,000 shares at the price of $1.12/share.

The ask price is always higher, or at the least equal to the bid price, and the difference between the two is known as the *spread*. The spread can therefore be seen as an indicator of price volatility where high spread values denote high levels of volatility in the stock price.

From an investment perspective, the bid and ask price are of little significance to trading decisions when access to this information is not provided instantaneously. In the event where this data stream is more frequently updated, the bid and ask price allow investors to anticipate the prospective intraday price direction of the stock (albeit not fully deterministically).

Monitoring the ask and bid prices on a stock quote can be distracting and sometimes even impossible when the stock price is changing rapidly. Instead of observing discrete-time values of ask and bid offers and monitoring the corresponding spread, investors are encouraged to monitor intraday price and volume charts which visualize the behavior of the stock in a scheme that is easier to interpret and act upon efficiently.

1-5-9. Estimated Metrics of Stock Quotes

The metrics presented in the previous paragraphs represent factual information that is mathematically accurate and free of speculation. However, in addition to this factual data, stock quotes also include information that normally reflects estimates and predictive views of analysts and advisory firms. Among these estimates are the

1-year Target Estimate and the estimated EPS value (Earnings per Share).

These metrics are only anticipated values, which are either estimated by analysts or predicted by market models. Short-term investment decisions should not rely on these estimates as a prime source of guidance as their accuracy is always subject to errors. As a matter of fact, if the 1-year target estimate was an accurate metric, one would think that buying shares into a stock whose current price is lower than the 1-year price estimate would be an easy venue to profit. However, this is seldom the case, and investors are cautioned not to base short-term trading decisions on such estimates, but rather on the factual quote data discussed earlier in this section, as well as on market news.

1-6.   PRE-MARKET AND AFTER HOUR QUOTES

The main difference between regular quotes and pre-market and after-hour quotes is that the former are available for every public stock (including OTCs and Pink Sheets), irrespective of the company's size and average daily volume, while the latter may or may not be available, especially for those small corporations whose stocks trade on low daily volumes.

As a result, regular quotes are more encompassing and depict a detailed comprehensive picture of the stock and its quoted data. Conversely, the extended-hour quotes—when they are available—focus exclusively on a select number of data, namely on the share pricing, the share volume and the price change during the extended session.

From a trading perspective, pre-market quotes are more relevant to trading decisions than after-hour quotes. This is because the early hours precede the regular hours, and thus they exhibit a more significant impact on the performance of the stock during the subsequent regular session.

In fact, recurrent trends in early-hour trading activities can be recognized and potentially adopted by investors to anticipate the performance of the stock, and formulate buying and selling decisions during the first minutes of the regular session (such trends will be discussed later in Chapter 7). In comparison, the after-hour quotes exhibit a lesser significance, where the positive or negative performance of a stock during these extended after—hours is typically short-lived, and does not necessarily carry into the trading session of the following day.

1-7.   STOCK CHARTS

Stock charts differ from stock quotes in that they reflect a history of the stock data over a period of time which could span one day, or could extend to as far back as the initial public offering of the stock. The most common stock charts are the price and volume charts. These either reflect the history of the price and volume change over the course of the trading session and are known as daily charts, or the history of the opening and closing price of the stock, along with the total share volume at the end of every trading session for an extended time frame.

The sample illustration in Figure 1.4 depicts such charts which reflect price and volume data of a stock over a period of one year. As can be seen in this figure, in a stock chart, the horizontal axis represents the time scale (hours/days/months/years), while the vertical axis represents the data value (price ($)/volume (millions of shares)).

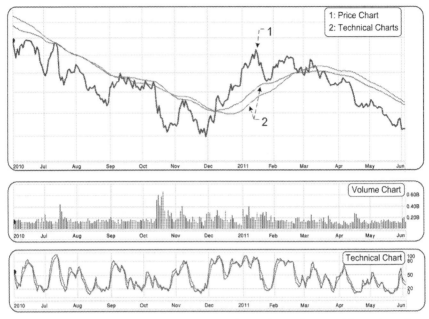

Figure 1.4. Sample price chart, corresponding volume chart, and few selected technical indicators for a period of one year (*Source:* finance.yahoo.com)

Stock charts constitute a fundamental source of information for market analysts and researchers. The data they graphically illustrate represents the core component of market models and technical analysis. Furthermore, because of the easy-to-read graphical scheme that stock charts employ, the data they present is as useful to investors as it is to market analysts. In fact, individual investors should always analyze stock charts before making any trading decisions, as the data they illustrate could have a significant impact on the outcome of investment decisions when analyzed properly.

In the context of chart analysis, price charts carry the most relevant information that can be analyzed to formulate appropriate trading positions. Price patterns in general tend to repeat themselves, making an understanding of the recurrent trends a very useful skill that a successful investor must possess in order to schedule correctly all buying and selling activities.

Such trends and price patterns will be discussed in more details in Chapters 4, 5, 6 and 7. Therefore, in this paragraph, the discussion will be limited to a sample visualization of price chart patterns that reflect the significance of extended price data (a 3 to 6 months price history is typically broad enough to enable the anticipation of the stock behavior on the short term).

Charts covering such time frame normally give a broad but important insight into the potential impact of a news release on the stock behavior. For example, a stock whose price has been rising during the previous six months may not respond as positively to a news release as another stock with the same news whose price has been losing value over the same period. This behavior goes back to the notion of undervaluation and overvaluation of a stock price presented earlier in section 1-5-5.

A stock whose price chart shows a decline in the previous three months (*e.g.* Figure 1.4) may very likely be undervalued, and therefore may respond to a positive news release in a more drastic way than a stock that has been gaining value over the same time frame.

The predictive value of such recurrent trends is well understood among investors on the stock market. For this reason, price and volume patterns are normally modeled with mathematical equations and plotted on the price or volume chart as technical indicators and overlays that simplify the noisy nature of the corresponding chart.

Figure 4 shows few of these overlays that are plotted directly on the price chart, or as individual indicators on separate graphs. There are many other charting techniques that traders rely on as visual aids when making trading decisions. The most popular of those are Candlestick and Kagi charts. A detailed discussion will be dedicated to stock charting techniques in *Part B* of this book.

1-8.   EARNINGS REPORT

Earnings reports represent a major quarterly event for public companies, where they are required by the regulatory commission (known as SEC) to release information about their performance at the end of every quarter (3 months), in a document known as earnings report or SEC filing.

These reports are in general published four times per year, on January, April, July and October. In addition to quarterly reports, companies publish supplementary annual statements summarizing the company's performance over its full fiscal year, typically from January to December.

Included in earnings reports are net profits or net losses from operations conducted over the previous quarter. This information is supplemented by budgetary data such as operating expenses, net sales and total revenues.

Earnings reports also publish information on Earnings per Share (EPS) attributed to stockholders, which represent the net profit of the company during the quarter, divided by the common outstanding shares of the stock. The EPS value may therefore be positive or negative, depending upon the company's operations and whether they resulted in profits or losses.

To establish a comparative statistical scheme, earnings reports compare the company's performance during every quarter to the performance during the previous quarter or the same quarter of the previous year. Annual reports are instead compared to the company's performance over the previous year.

These comparisons allow investors to interpret the performance of the company as percentages instead of monetary numbers. Indeed, earnings reports explicitly highlight these percentages in order to provide investors with a clear perspective about the direction of the company, and whether the operations of the quarter have increased or decreased the total revenues and profits.

To illustrate the relevance of percentile methodology in income statements, consider a company whose earnings report published a gross profit of $2 million over a given quarter. If this profit is not compared to the profit achieved in the previous quarter, the statement of *$2 million profit* may be ambiguous and difficult to interpret by investors.

However, if the company's earnings statement shows a $2 million profit compared to a $1 million profit over the previous quarter, such statement will unequivocally reflect positivity in the company's operations resulting in 100% increase in gross profit. Positive earnings reports such as these constitute a major investment opportunity for investors, since such earnings news may result in a significant positive increase in the stock value even on short-term basis during a single trading session.

Earnings reports are normally available as online documents to investors and are also distributed to shareholders. These reports are accompanied by conference calls scheduled by the company's executive board to discuss the business performance and forward operations outlook with stockholders.

1-9.   MISCELLANEOUS DEFINITIONS

In addition to the market terminologies and dynamics outlined in the previous paragraphs, some recurrent terms used on the market, in the news reports, and among traders and analysts also represent important vocabularies that investors should familiarize themselves with their meanings. The market connotations of some of these commonly used terms are highlighted in the following sections.

1-9-1. Bear Market/ Bull Market

Bear and *Bull* are two terminologies used to describe the direction of the market as a whole, or the direction and trends in individual sectors (such as oil, commodities, consumer products, *etc.*).

A bear market indicates a down-trend over a period of time reflecting investors' loss of confidence in the market. A bull market indicates an uptrend that reflects the increase in confidence and the optimism of investors in the market's positive prospects.

While there are no thresholds that define a bearish trend and a bullish trend, it is a common consensus among analysts to label a market as *bullish* when the major indices rise in value by 20% over a period of no less than two months. Conversely, a *bearish* market is indicated by a loss of 20% in the major indices over a period exceeding two months.

1-9-2. Support and Resistance

Support and resistance are two statistical concepts that represent a significant component of market models. By definition, *support* refers to the level at which the stock experiences more buying than selling activities, thus preventing the share price from dropping any further as the stock is losing value. When the stock finds support, it either remains flat, or bounces off towards positivity until it reaches a new resistance level.

Resistance on the other hand represents the opposite of support, where the selling activities outrun the buying activities, causing the share price to reach a saturation level beyond which the stock cannot maintain its positive trend. At this level, the stock is more likely to lose value and drop back to a lower price until it finds another support level, either during the same trading session or during a subsequent session.

Stock charts normally reveal a visual indication of support and resistance levels. However, predicting the onset of support or resistance—either visually or statistically through market models—represents a very challenging task especially when the market is marked by fear or a high level of volatility. Nonetheless, these two concepts are widely popular in technical analyses of the stock market, and are applied to the intraday behavior of a stock, as well as to extended charts.

1-9-3.   Penny Stock

A penny stock, as the name may indicate, is a stock whose share value is under \$1. These stocks exhibit unique behaviors on the market due to the high volatility rates associated with their trading activities, even under high trading volumes. For this reason, many brokerage firms and online resources recommend not to trade with penny stocks, and as a result, do not account for such stock activities in their daily reports and summaries.

While this may be a broad cautionary advice to avoid the drawbacks of high volatility, trading with penny stocks could in reality be very profitable, as long as the trading decisions are based on real and factual data released by the company, and not on scams and promotional advertisements that manipulate the market prospects of such stocks.

Penny stocks have the potential of generating large short-term profits when driven by positive news release. In fact, it is not uncommon that penny stocks double or even triple in value during one single trading session marked by a major news release. A sample example illustrating such performance is shown in Figure 1.5, where a penny stock gained 585% in value during one single trading session.

$2.12(March 3rd 4:00PM)

$0.31(March 3rd 9:30AM)

Feb Mar Apr May Jun Jul Aug Sep Oct Nov Dec

Figure 1.5. Extended chart of a penny stock showing a price percent increase of 585% during a single trading session (Opening Price: $0.31—Closing Price: $2.12) (*Source:* finance.yahoo.com)

The fact that penny stocks are significantly undervalued makes them very prone to considerable positivity as a reaction to an encouraging news release. This price increase, not only readjusts the share pricing, but also enables the stock to meet the continued listing requirements and avoid the risk of delisting which constitutes a further incentive for the stock to rally, especially when driven by insider trading (trading initiated by the brokers of the company themselves).

Thus, investors trading with penny stocks must understand the special dynamics of such stocks, and take advantage of positivity while remaining cautious about holding the stock for the long term. Trading penny stocks through online brokers may also be subject to additional commission fees, as well as to other trading restrictions, such as the nature of the orders that could be placed with penny stocks.

1-9-4.   Initial Public Offering (IPO)

An initial public offering represents the event during which a company offers its common shares for public trading, either for the very first time in the company's history, or for the second (or subsequent) time after a bankruptcy filing and restructuring of the company's operations under new management.

IPOs are normally undertaken in the objective of raising capital for the company in order to finance future growth activities. For this reason, IPOs constitute highly publicized events, especially when large corporations are entering the public market. Such events, in general, are marked by positive trading sessions which represent a unique opportunity for investors as enthusiasm and interest in the company's future outlook are high during the first trading sessions following the IPO.

1-9-5.   Stock Split/ Reverse Stock Split

A stock split increases the number of common shares in a company without affecting its market capitalization. For example, a company with 1,000 shares priced at $4 each has a market capitalization of 1,000×4=$4,000. In a stock split of 4-to-1, the number of shares is increased to 4,000 shares.

However, in order to maintain the same market cap, the share price is divided by four, to $1. This approach is pursued in order to attract smaller investors, and increase the buying activities in the stock, most notably for expensive stocks which are normally only affordable by institutional and privileged investors prior to the split.

On the other hand, a reverse stock split has the opposite effect of a stock split, where the number of shares is reduced and the share price is increased by the same amount in order to maintain the same market capitalization. A reverse stock split is done to attract investors who otherwise would not be interested in purchasing a cheap stock. For example, institutional investors such as hedge funds, normally maintain a policy where they limit their investments to stocks with shares priced above $5.

A stock priced under $5 would therefore execute a reverse split by an appropriate amount in order to attract such investors. A reverse split could also be executed with the objective of raising the share price of a penny stock in order to meet the listing requirements and avoid being delisted.

In general, a stock split is regarded as a sign of positivity in the company's operations, whereas a reverse split is often an indication of a dismal financial situation of the company. Thus, a reverse stock split is frequently accompanied by a decline in the share price, while a stock split has the opposite effect.

Stock quotes and charts in both cases are adjusted over the full public trading history of the company in order to reflect the decrease (or increase) in the share price as a consequence of the split (reverse split).

Chapter 2

ONLINE TRADING AND REGULATIONS

2-1. ONLINE BROKERAGE FIRMS

A brokerage firm is the institution that links investors to the stock market. Through a well regulated partnership, such institutions are authorized to conduct transactions on the behalf of their clientele in the form of buying and selling orders. These trade orders can be placed through the brokerage partner in multiple ways; over the phone, or more conveniently over the Internet.

In particular, Internet orders are becoming increasingly popular among investors because of their ease and speed of execution. Such orders are known as online transactions, and require an account with a registered Internet brokerage firm to place them.

In addition to executing client orders, brokerage firms can also act as investment advisers by providing counseling and advisory services to their clientele. These services are normally offered for a fee, and brokerage firms compete amongst themselves for client volume by reducing such fees. However, the bulk of the firms' profit is typically derived from commissions they collect on every buying and selling order they execute.

While commission rates vary from one firm to the other, it is a general custom to reduce such fees to a flat rate that is independent of the transaction volume. In this case, brokerage firms are more commonly known as discount brokers.

From an investment perspective, the selection of a brokerage partner represents a fundamental step in the process of online trading. Care must be taken in selecting the firm that offers the best services that fulfill the trading needs of investors. Making such choice must account for several factors that play a significant role in defining the capabilities of the firm. In particular, critical factors relating to the commission fees, the speed of order execution, and the frequency of quotes and share price updates in real-time must be given a careful consideration prior to making a broker selection.

2-1-1. Commission

The commission is the fee that investors pay to their brokers for executing a trade transaction resulting from a buying or a selling order. Rates normally vary from one brokerage firm to the other. However, because of the competition that exists between such firms, commission fees tend to be cheap and largely independent of the transaction volume.

In general, different commission fees apply to different trading orders. For instance, broker-assisted orders and phone orders tend to be more expensive than online orders. Moreover, in some cases, additional minor fees are appended to the flat commission rate when limit orders (refer to the definition of *limit orders* in section 2-3-6) are placed, such as when trading with penny stocks. These additional fees are assigned as a percentage (under 1% in general) of the transaction's monetary value.

Typically, the selection of a brokerage firm is influenced by the rate of trade commission. This is especially a main consideration when investors anticipate large trading activities with their online accounts, where multiple orders are placed, and subsequently multiple commissions are paid during every trading session. In the event where such online activity is not expected, commission rates may not weigh on the selection decision as significantly as other brokerage factors.

2-1-2. Execution Speed

The trade execution speed defines the rapidity at which an order placed online is executed from the time the order is submitted to the time the requested shares are either bought or sold. This execution speed represents a very important aspect of online trading as it determines the ultimate price at which requested shares can be either bought or sold.

Orders executed instantaneously have a significant probability of being completed at the desired price. In the event where a stock is marked by high price volatility at high trading volumes, such speed becomes very critical for two reasons. For one, it enables the execution of orders at the best price which is either at, or close to the price desired by the investor.

On the other hand, a high execution speed lessens the risk of free riding with cash accounts when orders are placed with no cash margin. In this case, a free ride resulting from a slow execution speed will have a negative impact on the investor's portfolio, and may lead to undesirable restrictions as imposed by online trade regulations (refer to the definition of *free riding* in section 2-4-2).

The execution speed, therefore, represents a critical factor that investors must consider when selecting a brokerage firm. In general, online brokers advertise for their execution speed by releasing statistical data that characterizes the quality of such service.

Care must be given in analyzing these statistics since the execution speed is never a constant parameter. In fact, the execution speed varies from one stock to the other, and depends significantly on the market liquidity. In the case of low liquidity, the execution time may extend up to a few minutes. On the other hand, this same execution time may be reduced to less than one second for the same stock at higher liquidity.

Typically, firms that are capable of achieving an average execution speed of less than 10 seconds are considered as reliable brokerage partners. In comparison, firms that tend to bundle orders, and execute them only a selected number of instances during every trading session do not constitute a prime choice for such partnership.

2-1-3.   Price Updates

Once a buying order is executed by the online brokerage firm and the requested shares are bought, the total value of these shares is updated as the stock price varies over the course of the trading session. Such updates are reflected in the share price and the total account value.

The update speed generally varies from one firm to the other. Ideally, the share price and the account value are updated instantaneously, and in parallel with the stock price fluctuations. However, these updates could be delayed by brokers for up to 15 minutes in some instances, depending upon the quality of their trading services.

The selection of a brokerage firm must take into account the frequency of share price updates. A high frequency gives the investors the opportunity to place a selling order at the *peak* price whenever such peak occurs. If the price updates are otherwise delayed, such opportunity may be long gone by the time price fluctuations are reflected in the total account value.

To illustrate the relevance of this aspect of instantaneous price updates, a sample scenario is highlighted in Figure 2.1 where the share price of a stock fluctuates significantly within a very short period of time during a regular trading session. As seen in this figure, a 77% increase (from $2.15 to $ 3.80) in share value occurred within a 2-minute time span, followed immediately by a 28% decrease (from $3.8 to $2.75) in value in the subsequent two minutes.

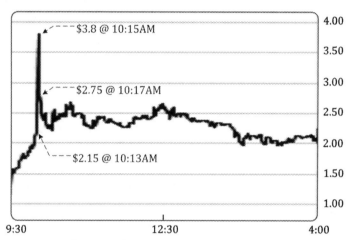

Figure 2.1. Intraday price chart showing a 77% increase, followed by a 28% decrease in share value within a total time span of 4 minutes
(*Source:* www.quotemedia.com)

The ability of the brokerage firm to provide instantaneous updates of the account value during price fluctuations such as the ones reflected in Figure 2.1, represents a key element in enabling investors to place a selling order at the peak price (*i.e.* at 10:15 AM in this case). However, such opportunity would be missed if the price updates are delayed even by few minutes. For this reason, the frequency of price updates represents another critical factor in the selection of a brokerage firm, since this service exhibits a direct influence on the potentiality of profit maximization during selling transactions.

2-1-4. Quotes, Charts and Market News

Market tools represent another factor for consideration during the selection of an online brokerage partner. These tools consist of market data in the form of quotes, charts and relevant news which together constitute the foundation of stock trading.

All brokerage firms, in general, provide quoting and charting services to their registered clientele. The key difference however between one firm and the other lies in the update rates and the level of quoting and charting details. Update rates for instance can vary from a few seconds, up to 20 minutes in some cases.

Typically, firms that provide instantaneous share price updates also provide quote and chart updates at the same rate. However, unlike account value updates which can only be provided by the brokerage partner, instantaneous quotes and charts can be found on open-access web pages for almost all stocks that trade publically on the floors of NYSE, NASDAQ and AMEX. These open-access tools will be discussed in more details in Chapter 3.

In the same direction of share pricing and execution speed, the update frequency of charts and quotes represents a very critical aspect that defines the quality of brokerage services. This is because this aspect weighs considerably on spontaneous investment decisions, where fast update frequencies enable investors to react instantaneously to impromptu trends in the market. Such reaction would be impossible if charts and quotes are delayed by 15 minutes.

To visualize the importance of fast quoting and charting update rates and their impact on trading decisions, a sample illustration is shown in Figure 2.2 where a stock gained 54% in share value (from $1.35 to $2.09) during the first 11 minutes of a trading session, before dropping to a lower threshold. If the chart was delayed by 15 minutes, the stock price would effectively be at $1.99/share by the time an investor gets to spot it. This means that all margin for profit during the fast morning ascent will be missed because of this delay, and an uncalculated buying order placed at $1.99/share (at 9:45 AM) would have resulted in intraday loses as the stock never managed to establish a new high during the remainder of the session.

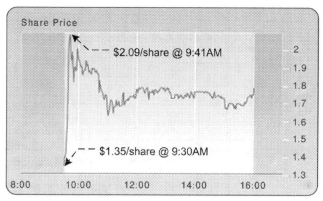

Figure 2.2. Sample chart showing the fast momentum of a stock increasing by 54% in share value during the first 11 minutes of a trading session
(*Source:* www.nasdaq.com)

2-1-5. Account Maintenance Fee

Some brokerage firms impose maintenance fees that apply to client accounts on quarterly or annual basis. This fee is either a flat rate, or represents a percentage of the account value.

Although such fees are being dismissed by firms in order to attract customers and compete against each other, some firms still maintain this practice where they tend to *camouflage* it within their services without the prior knowledge of their clientele. In this case, investors must be careful about partnering with such firms, and must question the existence of any hidden fees that may not be openly disclosed by the selected broker.

2-2. ACCOUNT TYPES

Once an online brokerage partner is selected with services that satisfy the trading aspirations of the investor, an account must be created with this firm in order to enable the placement and execution of trade orders. In general, there are several types of online accounts that investors may be able to create with their brokerage partner; the most common of these are cash accounts and margin accounts.

2-2-1. Cash Account

In a cash account, investors are required to either have enough money to cover the expenses of a buying order, or be able to deposit the required money within three days of the purchasing transaction (such period is known as *settlement time* and will be discussed in more details in section 2-4-1).

For example, a cash account with $1,000 enables an investor— mathematically—to place a buying order of at most 1,000 shares in a stock trading at $1.00/share. In reality, one must also consider the commission fee, and leave a small cash cushion in the account to avoid free riding in case the order was executed at a slightly higher price than the desired one (depending upon the volatility of the stock). These considerations slightly reduce the buying capability of online investors, and allow them to purchase an effective stake that is relatively smaller than the mathematical maximum.

From a trading perspective, cash accounts represent the safest form of online stock trading, where investors are not taking any risks in leveraging their buying capabilities through borrowed money made possible with margin accounts.

Novice investors are thus most encouraged to trade with cash accounts by depositing money, and waiting for the proceeds of a selling order to settle before placing another buying order. Depositing money into cash accounts is typically subject to a 10-day restriction period during which the deposited money cannot be used for placing any purchasing orders.

2-2-2. Margin Account

Unlike cash accounts where the trading potential of investors is delimited by the amount of cash available in the account, a margin account enables investors to leverage their purchasing capabilities by borrowing money from their brokers. In this process, the account value in cash and securities is used as the guaranteed assets (or collateral) for a line of credit that the brokerage firm extends to its clientele with margin accounts to enable them to buy more stocks.

Borrowing money from brokers is typically subject to high interest rates. This means that investors have to generate larger profits in margin accounts to cover the additional expenses incurred from such interest rates. As this infers, margin buying could be far riskier than cash buying as the fees are higher and the leverage has the potential of magnifying losses on purchased stocks.

To illustrate this concept of leverage magnification with an example, consider an investor with a margin account of $1,000 in cash value. If this money was used to buy a certain number of shares in a stock that subsequently loses 10% of its value, the investor would incur a monetary loss of $100.

However, if the investor borrows an additional $9,000 from the broker to purchase shares in the same stock which later loses 10% of its value, the loss incurred with this leverage becomes $1,000 instead of $100. This means that the original cash value of the account would be wiped out completely because of the leverage.

This practice of margin trading represents a crafted tool that only experienced investors can employ successfully to maximize their profit. These investors normally have the ability to spot profitable trends in a stock (possibly based on inside information), and borrow money to maximize the number of shares they can buy in this stock in order to leverage their profit. Such techniques are usually employed on short-term basis, such as for few minutes or for a full trading session (at the most) in order to reduce interest rates. For novice investors however, these practices are risky and must not be adopted until enough confidence in understanding market trends is established.

2-3.   ONLINE TRADING TOOLS

2-3-1.   Trading Long

Long trading denotes the traditional form of stock investment where an investor buys shares at a certain price and later sells them to cash the profit after they appreciate in value. Most investors adopt this trading strategy in order to minimize the risk exposure associated with the trading process.

Long positions also offer the potential of generating more than 100% return on stock investments. This is not possible with other forms of trading, such as short positions, where profit is made if the stock loses value. In such case, the maximum profit that an investor can generate on short trades cannot exceed a theoretical 100% as a share value cannot depreciate to below $0.

2-3-2. Trading Short

In short trading, investors generate profit by bidding on the fact that a given stock will lose value during the time they are holding it. These trading techniques are mostly adopted to generate profit during a period of bear markets where stock prices are falling.

The process of short trading involves the broker lending a certain number of shares to the investor who is bidding on the potentiality of the stock losing value before actually buying the shares. To illustrate this concept with an example, consider an investor short buying 100 shares of a stock priced at $5. In this process, the broker is actually lending the proceeds of the 100 shares ($500) to the investor where the amount is credited to his/her account.

If the price of the stock falls to $4/share, the investor buys these shares back at $400, returns them to the lender and keeps the profit ($100) in the account. This process is known as short buying or buying to cover.

However, if the price of the share goes up to $6, the short buyer would have lost the bid and will have to pay an extra $100 to the lender if he/she decides to buy the shares at $6. Such decision is contingent with interest assigned to borrowed money, where the rates increase proportionally with the duration of time during which the investor holds the stocks of the short trade.

As can be inferred from the previous example, short trading involves more risk than long trading where the former technique is normally reserved to experienced investors. Novice investors on the other hand are in no means encouraged to short stocks, even during a period of bear markets. In fact, one should always remember that bear markets don't necessarily mean that long trades are not profitable or even possible. For small investors, such opportunities are always present with small-cap companies that exhibit a minor influence on the direction of the market.

2-3-3.   Buying to Cover

Covering a short trade is the process where the investor buys the original number of shares in order to close an open position resulting from a short sell. This covering process occurs whenever the investor speculates that the price of the stock will rise, thus triggering a buying action in order to limit losses as profit on short trades can only be made if the price falls.

Covering is not applicable to long trades where a buy action precedes a sell action. It is rather only applicable to short trades where a sell order is first initiated, and then followed by a buying order to cover the short.

2-3-4.   All or None (AON)

AON is a condition imposed by investors on their brokers when placing a buying or a selling order. Under this condition, brokers are instructed to execute the order only if all shares are either bought or sold at once.

For example, an AON buying order of 1,000 shares can only be executed if all 1,000 shares can be bought together at the same price. If this condition is not imposed, the 1,000-shares buying order can be executed on multiple consecutive instances. This may result in shares being bought in batches at different prices depending upon the stock's volatility rate, and may potentially incur the payment of multiple commissions for every intermediate order executed separately.

For example, a non-AON buying order of 1,000 shares placed on a stock trading at $1.50/share may be executed on three different occasions, where the first 400 shares are bought at $1.50, the next 500 shares at $1.52, and the last 100 shares at $1.53. Conversely, an AON order remains open until a buyer is willing to buy the 1,000 shares all together. If such opportunity does not present itself, the AON order will not be executed and will ultimately be canceled at the end of the trading session.

From an investment perspective, there are no obvious advantages for an AON order over a non-AON order, except for the additional commission that may be incurred for a non-AON order, and the risk that may be associated with an *AON market* order where the stock share may reach an undesirable price by the time the order is executed.

To avoid such risks—despite the possibility of paying multiple commissions—investors are encouraged to trade with non-AON orders in most cases unless the liquidity of the stock is high.

2-3-5. Market Order

A market order is the most fundamental form of online transactions, where the investor instructs the broker to execute the order immediately, at the best price available but without specifying such price.

By removing any restrictions on the broker, a market order is more likely to be executed even at low liquidity. This however comes at the expense of the final price, where in the case of low liquidity, such price may be somewhat offset from the anticipated one. A market order expires at the end of the trading session if it remains unexecuted.

2-3-6. Limit Order

In a limit order, the desired buying or selling price is specified by the investor when placing the order. For example, a selling order of 100 shares at a limit price of $2.25 can only be executed if the share price reaches $2.25 or higher. Thus, a limit order defines the minimum price at which a specified number of shares should be sold, or conversely, the maximum price at which the requested shares should be bought.

In a non-AON limit order where not all shares can be sold at the limit price (or better), only those shares that can be traded are executed. The remaining shares will be held, either for a later execution when another limit-price opportunity presents itself, or until the order on the remaining shares is canceled by the investor. A limit order can also remain active until a specific date determined by the investor.

The advantage of a limit order is that the price of the shares is *at worse* as desired by the investor once the order is executed. This is unlike a market order where the final price represents a feat of fortune that depends on the stock liquidity. The risk however is that the desired price may never be attained by the stock, and that investors may have to downgrade the limit price in order to sell the shares eventually.

While limit orders are typically optional, they are rather imposed mandatorily by some brokerage firms when placing orders on penny stocks. In such case, limit orders may be more expensive than market orders, where an additional minor commission fee is appended to the flat rate that is normally assigned to market orders.

2-3-7. Stop Order/ Stop Limit Order

A stop order is triggered with a buy action when the stock price exceeds the specified stop price, or with a sell action when the stock price falls below the stop price. Stop orders are frequently employed when investors are concerned about the direction of the stock when they are unable to monitor such movement.

For example, a sell stop order may be placed on a stock trading at $3.40 if the stock price falls below $3.20. The difference between the current price and the stop price represents the percentage that the investor is willing to loose in account value when bidding on the stock to go higher.

If the stock falls below the stop price, the selling order is executed as a market order at the best price available below the stop price (without specifying such price). For instance, the order in the prior example can be executed at $3.19 once the price falls below the stop threshold of $3.20.

A stop limit order on the other hand is identical to a stop order, with the exception that once the stop price is reached, the order will be executed as a limit order instead of a market order. In such case, the investor must also specify a limit price in addition to the initial stop price.

Similar to a limit order, a stop order can remain active for the whole trading session if not executed. It can also remain active until a specified date or until it is canceled by the investor.

2-3-8. Trailing Stop Order/ Trailing Stop Limit Order

A trailing stop order is placed with a stop amount that generates a moving activation price. This amount is either entered as a monetary value, or as a percentage of the maximum price the share attains over the period during which the trailing stop order is active. The fact that the activation price—or the stop price—is automatically adjustable as a function of the share price enables investors to benefit from any subsequent opportunity in price hikes in order to maximize profit. Such opportunity will not be available through a simple stop order.

To illustrate the dynamics of a trailing stop order with an example, consider a stock with a share price of $2.50. If a trailing stop order with a trailing stop amount of $0.50 is placed on this stock, such order will not be executed unless the share price falls below $2.00.

However, if the stock price jumps over a period of one week (for example) to a maximum of $4.50, the stop price will be automatically adjusted to $4.00 instead of $2.00. Subsequently, if the share price drops back to $4.00, the stop order will be triggered and the specified shares will be sold as a market order at the next best price, *i.e.* at $3.95 for example.

However, if the same transaction was entered as a stop order instead of a trailing stop order, and that the stock jumped to $4.50 before it started declining again, the stop threshold will still be set at $2.00. This means that the investor will lose all opportunities to benefit from the stock price rising from $2.50 to $4.50, and can only sell the shares automatically when the price falls back to the initial stop price of $2.00.

A trailing stop limit order is identical to a trailing stop order with the exception that the former is executed as a limit instead of a market order. As such, entering a trailing stop limit order requires the determination of a limit price in addition to the stop price. The activation of a trailing order can also extend for a whole trading session unless the order is executed, or until a specified date unless the order is canceled by the investor.

2-4.   ONLINE TRADING REGULATIONS

The practice of trading stocks online is governed by trade regulations imposed by the United States Federal Reserve Board. These regulations define the requirements and policies under which stocks and other securities are traded publically in the United States, and delineate the obligations that investors and brokers should fulfill towards one another when exchanging such securities.

Of all federal trade regulations, *Regulation T* represents the most relevant policy that governs stock trading activities with cash and margin accounts. Under this regulation, cash accounts are subject to a hold period known as a *settlement time*, during which proceeds resulting from a stock sell cannot be used to place another buying order until after the funds have settled.

For margin accounts, *Regulation T* defines collateral requirements, and controls the risk associated with margin trading by limiting the amount of credit that brokers can extend to their clientele in order to leverage their purchasing capabilities.

The current initial margin in the United States is 50%, and credit cannot be extended to any account with less than $2,000 in market value according to *Regulation T*. This means that an investor borrowing money on a margin account must have at least 50% of the total purchasing amount available in the account as collateral, in the form of cash or other securities (such as stocks) that could be sold at any time to cover the margin.

For example, an investor having $3,000 in cash in a margin account can borrow—at most—an additional $3,000 to place a total order of 6,000 shares on a stock trading at $1/share. By increasing the initial margin requirements to a higher percentage, the regulatory board can limit the purchasing capabilities of investors trading with borrowed money, thereby reducing the risk of loss magnification through leveraging.

Any violations of these requirements and the trading terms defined by *Regulation T* are subject to trade restrictions imposed by brokers on cash and margin accounts. These violations are commonly known as *free rides*, or *freeriding*.

2-4-1. Settlement Time/Date

The settlement time denotes the period at the end of which the broker must pay for the stocks sold by the investor. In the United States, this period is defined by *Regulation T* as three days for stocks and one day for options and mutual funds.

Settled funds are thus those funds that are deposited into a cash account and have cleared the 10-day restriction period, or the funds that result from the proceeds of a selling order that has cleared the 3-day settlement period. Such funds can be used to purchase stocks at any time, with the freedom to sell them back at liberty without any violation of the trading regulations.

For example, if an investor buys 200 shares of a stock trading at $4/share on Monday at 10:00 AM and sells them back at 3:00 PM of the same day at $5/share, the proceeds ($1,000) of this transaction will settle on Thursday of the same week.

By Thursday, the investor can use the settled $1,000 to place another buying order of 500 shares on another stock trading at $2/share and sell them back on the same day—or later—without incurring the risk of a free ride.

Such techniques of buying stocks with settled funds represent the safest and most desirable forms of stock trading with cash accounts, and enables investors to maintain a *healthy* portfolio that is free of any trading restrictions.

Unsettled funds on the other hand are those funds that originate from the proceeds of a selling order which has not cleared the 3-day settlement period. These funds cannot be used to place a new buying order until after the settlement date of the original selling transaction. However, if unsettled funds were used to place a new buying order, selling the newly purchased securities prior to the settlement date of the original purchase will result in a trade violation and subsequently in a free ride.

2-4-2. Free Ride

Free riding, as defined earlier, refers to any action that violates the trading terms and requirements dictated by *Regulation T*. Most commonly, these violations occur with cash accounts when the unsettled proceeds of a selling order are used to place a new buying order which is subsequently sold prior to the settlement time.

To illustrate this concept with an example in reference to the timeline depicted in Figure 2.3, consider an investor placing a buying order of

2,000 shares on a stock trading at $3/share on Tuesday at 9:30 AM, for a total transaction value of $6,000.

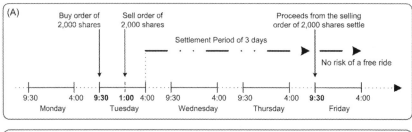

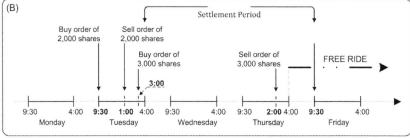

Figure 2.3. Timeline showing, (A) the settlement period following a buy and a sell order with settled funds, (B) a free ride originating from a buy and sell order placed during the settlement period

Because the order was placed with settled funds, the investor sells the 6,000 shares back at 1:00 PM of the same day at a price of $3.30/share generating $6,600 in unsettled funds. These funds will have a settlement period of three days after the trading day of Tuesday, which means that the proceeds of $6,600 should not be used to place another buying order prior to Friday (Figure 2.3(A)).

However, if the investor spots another opportunity on Tuesday at 3:00 PM and decides to buy 3,000 shares of a stock trading at $2.20/share for a total value of $6,600, those 3,000 shares cannot be sold prior to Friday because the order was placed with the unsettled funds derived from Tuesday's selling order. This means that the investor will have to hold the 3,000 shares throughout the remainder of Tuesday's trading session and into the full sessions of Wednesday and Thursday.

However, if the stock starts losing value on Thursday and drops down to $1.9/share forcing the investor to sell the 3,000 shares at 2:00 PM, such action will not only cause the investor to lose $900 in account value (3,000shares × $1.9/share = $5,700), but will also initiate a free ride violation on the account (Figure 2.3(B)).

Free riding also occurs during fast moving markets where investors are using all cash in their accounts to place buying orders on stocks marked by high volatility (this is the reason for which investors must leave a cash cushion in their cash accounts in order to offset any free ride violation that may result from fast moving markets).

For example, consider an investor with $1,500 of settled funds (in a cash account) placing a buy market-order of 950 shares on a stock trading at $1.50/share, on the premise that the order will be executed at or near the current price of $1.50/share ($1,425 total transaction value).

However, because of high volatility, the order was instead executed at $1.70/share for a total transaction value of $1,615 (excluding commission). This means that the investor indirectly borrowed $190 (1,615-1,425) from the broker in order to cover the additional expenses resulting from the order being executed at a higher price than the original share price of $1.50.

In such case, despite the initial intentions of the investor to stay within the bounds of the account's monetary capabilities, the fact that the account is not approved for margin and that the transaction value—at the time of execution—was larger than the total cash available in the account, results directly in a free ride violation.

When three free ride violations occur, the broker is instructed by *Regulation T* to freeze the account for 90 days. This means that investors can still trade with frozen accounts, but they can only do so using settled funds, as the ability to trade with unsettled funds will be completely restricted. When these restrictions apply, placing orders such as the Tuesday's buying order of 3,000 shares in the first example of this section will become impossible.

If on the other hand, another free ride violation occurs once the freeze is lifted off of the account after the 90-day restriction period, Regulation *T* instructs that cash accounts will be restricted from trading with unsettled funds on permanent basis. This means that only trades initiated with settled funds will be possible subsequently.

Chapter 3

WEB RESOURCES FOR STOCK TRADING

3-1.   ONLINE RESOURCES FOR MARKET DATA

Trading stocks online requires up-to-the-second information about the movement of the market as a whole, and more specifically, the movement of individual stocks including those with small market capitalization whose influence on the market direction is minimal. This information represents an important component of stock trading, since it serves as a daily market compass that enables investors to single out the few stocks whose intraday market data shows promising signs of profit.

Online investors depend on their brokerage partners for free access to market data and analysis tools in order to support the formulation of daily trading positions. All brokerage firms, in general, provide these services to their registered clientele in the form of charts, quotes, news and top gainers and top losers lists. However, the rate at which this information is updated throughout the intraday session varies from one firm to the other, along with the level of details provided in the quoting and charting services.

Nevertheless, due to the high public interest in the stock market; intraday market data, real-time data, and extended charts are all available on open access web pages such as *Yahoo.com* and *Nasdaq. com*. This makes market data accessible to everyone interested in the stock market, including those who are not involved in any trading activities, and those who do not possess any trading accounts with an online brokerage firm.

The information provided by such open-access web sources is updated at a high enough rate, and thus can be used to supplement the market data provided by brokerage firms. It can equally be used as a primary source of data and news for individuals interested in market analysis and research activities.

3-2.   TOP GAINERS LIST

Formulating a buying position on day-to-day basis can be influenced by many implicit and explicit factors. These factors range from analysis reports released by independent research firms, to insider trading where the unusual movement of a stock is not supported explicitly by a news release.

One of the most reliable sources of information that enables investors to formulate a daily trading position is the *Top Gainers List*. This list provides an initial insight into the daily market movers, by singling out the best performers of the day in a sorted list that is updated frequently throughout every trading session. The Top Gainers List therefore represents a statistical table that sorts—in a descending order—up to twenty-five stocks based on the percentage increase in corresponding share value during every trading session.

The stocks featured on the Top Gainers List could correspond to the whole US stock market, or to individual NYSE, NASDAQ and AMEX markets. A sample of such list is presented in Figure 3.1 for stocks belonging to the US market as a whole.

Symbol	Name	Last Trade	Change	Volume
US NASDAQ AMEX NYSE				
AHCI	Allied HealthCare International	3.82 Jul 29	↑ 1.37 (55.92%)	24,659,575
CRMBU	57TH Street General Acquisition	3.82 Jul 29	↑ 5.34 (36.58%)	100
ZOLL	Zoll Medical Corporation	69.66 Jul 29	↑ 14.27 (25.76%)	1,674,612
STMP	Stamps.com Inc.	16.75 Jul 29	↑ 3.07 (22.44%)	437,881
SIFY	Sify Technologies Limited	4.90 Jul 29	↑ 0.88 (21.89%)	3,769,687
HOVNP	Hovnanian Enterprises Inc	4.26 Jul 29	↑ 0.72 (20.34%)	10,380
CNAM	China Armco Metals, Inc. Common	1.60 Jul 29	↑ 0.26 (19.40%)	139,478
MXWL	Maxwell Technologies, Inc.	16.87 Jul 29	↑ 2.74 (19.39%)	689,263
ACFN	Acorn Energy, Inc.	4.84 Jul 29	↑ 0.77 (18.92%)	769,928
CPSI	Computer Programs and Systems,	73.45 Jul 29	↑ 10.96 (17.54%)	417,454

Figure 3.1. Sample Top Gainers List with 10 best performing stocks from the whole US stock market, sorted in a decreasing order of price percent change (*Source:* finance.yahoo.com/gainers)

The stocks of the Top Gainers list may vary from one source to another. In some cases, only stocks trading above $1/share appear on the list. In other cases, cheaper stocks—including pennies—are given a higher priority than other more expensive stocks. Pink Sheets and Over-The-Counter (OTC) stocks are normally not considered for the Top Gainers List.

In all cases however, analyzing the Top Gainers List represents a primary step that is fundamental for short-term day trading. This is because the Top Gainers List enables online investors to restrict their focus to a selected number of stocks which are exhibiting the best positive trends during every session. Such stocks are normally the ones that offer viable opportunities for profit during the day, and thus must be given a higher attention by investors, especially those trading on short-term strategies.

In this context, inspecting the Top Gainers List at the beginning (9:30 AM) and throughout the intraday trading session should become a routine procedure by online investors who expect to place a buying order during the session. The challenge however is to find access to a list that is updated at an instantaneous rate in line with the rapid change in the market.

In general, most Top Gainers Lists are delayed by at least fifteen minutes, including those offered by some brokerage firms. This means that investors relying on the Top Gainers List as a trading compass may see their buying opportunities long gone by the time the price percent change updates are reflected on the list.

Nevertheless, market research shows that while some open-access Top Gainers Lists are delayed by 15 minutes, the ranking of their featured stocks is in fact updated instantaneously throughout the intraday session in accordance with the market movement. The delay is rather only evidenced in the display of the price percent change and other related information.

To illustrate this process with an example, consider the sample Top Gainers List shown in Figure 3.2. This figure represents an excerpt from the first update which was retrieved at 9:30 AM, *i.e.* at the beginning of a given trading session. In this list, it is obvious that the ranking of the featured stocks is not explicitly based on the percent change, as the latter is not yet displayed on the list (all percent changes are 0.00%).

However, if one inspects the early performance of each of the stocks featured on this list, it becomes clear that the ranking is indeed done according to the corresponding price change (%) which will not be displayed until 15 minutes later. This implicit price change employed to rank the stocks featured in Figure 3.2 is summarized in Table 3.1, where the early morning percent gain is reflected in green. Note that the ranking of the symbols in Figure 3.2 is compliant with the decreasing order of the price percent change of the corresponding stocks in Table 3.1, which explains the specific ranking scheme featured on the Top Gainers List of Figure 3.2.

US	NASDAQ	AMEX	NYSE		
Symbol	Name	Last Trade	Change	Volume	
SPWRB	SunPower Corporation	15.78 Apr 28	0.00 (0.00%)	433,648	
SPWRA	SunPower Corporation	16.12 Apr 28	0.00 (0.00%)	569,104	
NTGR	NETGEAR, Inc.	34.00 Apr 28	0.00 (0.00%)	14,301	
STBC	State Bancorp, Inc.	10.96 Apr 28	0.00 (0.00%)	1,000	
GBLI	Global Indemnity plc	21.78 Apr 28	0.00 (0.00%)	0	
SIMO	Silicon Motion Technology Corpo	11.16 Apr 28	0.00 (0.00%)	4,915	
ASGN	On Assignment, Inc.	9.21 Apr 28	0.00 (0.00%)	3,300	

Figure 3.2. A sample Top Gainers List at 9:30 AM where stocks are ranked based on an implicit price percent change. Actual values will be reflected 15 minutes later (*Source:* finance.yahoo.com/gainers)

Table 3.1. Explicit price percent change of the stocks featured in Figure 3.2, highlighting the corresponding ranking scheme

Stock Symbol	Explicit Price Percent Change[*]
SPWRB	SunPower Corporation (NasdaqGS: SPWRB) REAL-TIME 21.90 ↑ 6.12 (38.78%) 9:31AM EDT
SPWRA	SunPower Corporation (NasdaqGS: SPWRA) REAL-TIME 22.23 ↑ 6.11 (37.90%) 9:31AM EDT
NTGR	NETGEAR, Inc. (NasdaqGS: NTGR) REAL-TIME 41.58 ↑ 7.58 (22.29%) 9:31AM EDT
STBC	State Bancorp, Inc. (NasdaqGM: STBC) REAL-TIME 13.11 ↑ 2.15 (19.62%) 9:30AM EDT

GBLI	**Global Indemnity plc** (NasdaqGS: GBLI)
	REAL-TIME **25.48** ↑ 3.70 (16.99%) 9:31AM EDT
SIMO	**Silicon Motion Technology Corpo** (NasdaqGS: SIMO)
	REAL-TIME **12.99** ↑ 1.83 (16.40%) 9:32AM EDT
ASGN	**On Assignement, Inc.** (NasdaqGS: ASGN)
	REAL-TIME **10.66** ↑ 1.45 (15.74%) 9:33AM EDT

*Source: finance.yahoo.com

Furthermore, such Top Gainers Lists can also be used as a compass to react to any impromptu changes in the market throughout every trading session, where a sudden hike in a stock not previously featured on the list can be directly spotted, even if the corresponding price percent change is not reflected immediately.

To visualize this process, Figure 3.3 shows a scenario where a stock is inexplicably sorted among the top five stocks of the day's Top Gainers List at around 1:30 PM. While the price percent change shows no reasons for this ranking, an inspection of the stock's intraday chart reveals a sudden spike of 27% in the price due to a recent news release.

Because of this abundance of information that can be extracted from the Top Gainers List, online investors (trading long) should employ this tool as a market compass in order to spot profitable trends in positively moving stocks. These trends can be highlighted at the beginning of the trading session where the liquidity in the market is at its peak, or throughout the trading session where a late news release could generate significant gains, with the possibility of extending the upward trend into the following trading sessions (this depends upon the connotations carried by the news driving such stocks which will be discussed in more details in Chapters 4 and 5).

US	NASDAQ	AMEX	NYSE			
Symbol	Name		Last Trade	Change		Volume
ZIP	Zipcar, Inc.		28.37 1:09PM EDT	⬆ 10.37 (57.61%)		8,546,613
CHINA	CDC Corporation		3.10 1:09PM EDT	⬆ 0.71 (29.71%)		5,724,933
PEDH	Peoples Educational Holdings		1.50 12:25PM EDT	⬆ 0.37 (32.74%)		25,451
NEP	China North East Petroleum Hold		4.31 1:09PM EDT	⬆ 1.06 (32.62%)		1,516,703
ACOR	Acorda Therapeutics, Inc.		21.42 1:09PM EDT	0.00 (0.00%)		146,060
OXBT	Oxygen Biotherapeutics, Inc.		2.04 12:39PM EDT	⬆ 0.33 (19.30%)		167,546

Real Time Stock Quotes: Acorda Therapeutics, Inc. (ACOR)

4/11/2011 1:27:08 PM Market Open	
ACOR's NASDAQ Last Sale	
27.24 5.82 ⬆ 27.17%	
NLS Volume	Previous Close
848,404	**$ 21.42**
Today's High	Today's Low
$ 28.1100	**$ 21.1700**
52 Wk High	52 Wk Low
$ 40.48	**$ 20.43**
NASDAQ Official Price	
Open Price/Date	ClosePrice/Date
$ 21.25	**$ 21.42**
Apr 14, 2011	**Apr 13, 2011**
1y Target Est	
$ 27	

Figure 3.3. A sudden change in the Top Gainers List at 1:30 PM of a given trading session, correlated with the corresponding price hike of the newly featured stock (*Sources:* finance.yahoo.com/gainers & www.nasdaq.com)

3-3. TOP LOSERS LIST/ TOP MOST ACTIVE LIST

In addition to the Top Gainers List, daily market movers are also aggregated into a Top Losers List and a Top Most Active List.

The Top Losers List represents the opposite of the Top Gainers list, where the ranking scheme features those stocks whose share value drops the most during every trading session. Such list is mainly employed by short traders who derive profit from negative trends by bidding on losing stocks to lose even more value.

The Top Most Active list, however, sorts stocks based on share volume, irrespective of the price percent change. Because the price change is not taken into consideration, the Top Most Active List often always features those stocks that correspond to the largest corporations in the United States which are commonly known as *Blue Chip Stocks.*

This makes the Top Most Active List irrelevant to the trading strategies of small investors, which are driven by the price percent change more so than the share volume (provided that the volume is high enough to supply the required liquidity).

For this reason, small investors are namely encouraged to employ the Top Gainers List as a market compass to formulate buying positions, and not the Top Losers or the Top Most Active Lists whose ranking schemes are mainly irrelevant to the portfolios of such investors.

3-4.   OPEN-ACCESS WEB QUOTES

Stock quotes represent a tabular list of market data that defines specific metrics about a given stock such as the share price and the share volume. These quotes are normally offered as a free service by brokerage firms to their registered clientele, or can alternatively be found on open-access web pages. A sample illustration of such quotes is shown in Figure 3.4, for the same stock quoted by two different open-access web sources.

Last Trade:	2.05	Day's Range:	1.50-2.13
Trade Time:	Aug 5	52wk Range:	0.88-6.49
Change:	⬆ 0.55 (36.66%)	Volume:	21,599
Prev Close:	1.50	Avg Vol (3m):	50,885
Open:	1.51	Market Cap:	8.10M
Bid:	1.01x100	P/E (ttm):	13.58
Ask:	2.34x400	EPS (ttm):	0.15
1y Target Est:	N/A	Div & Yield:	N/A (N/A)

Last Sale	$ 2.05
Change Net/%	0.5499 △ 36.66%
Best Bid/Ask	N/A / N/A
1y Target Est:	N/A
Today's High/Low	$ 2.13 / $ 1.50
Share Volume	21,599
50 Day Avg. Daily Volume	62,319
Previous Close	$ 1.5001
52 Wk High / Low	$ 6.49 / $ 0.88
Shares Outstanding	3,952,000
Market Value of Listed Security	$ 8,101,600
P/E Ratio	29.29
Forward P/E (1yr)	N/A
Earnings Per Share	$ 0.07
Annualized Dividend	N/A
Ex Dividend Date	N/A
Dividend Payment Date	N/A
Current Yield	N/A
Beta	-0.58

Figure 3.4. Two quotes and summary data for the same stock retrieved from two different web sources (*Top Source:* finance.yahoo.com, *Bottom Source:* www.nasdaq.com)

Web quotes and corresponding summary data are generally delayed by 15 to 20 minutes. This differs from quoting services offered by some brokerage firms where quotes are updated instantaneously. However, investors basing their trading positions on open-access web quotes should not be affected by this delay.

This is because variations in many quote metrics such as the average daily volume and the market cap exhibit an insignificant impact on the intraday performance of the stock, and subsequently on the investor's trading decisions. For instance, if a stock with a market cap of $9.0 million at 9:30 AM is marked by high buying activities during a given trading session, its market cap will rise in parallel with this activity to reflect the increase in the share price, ending the day at $11.0 million.

However, the history of this increase in the market cap, whether it was furnished to the investor immediately, or whether it was delayed throughout the session, does not effectively change the dynamics of the stock and the subsequent investor's position in any means possible. Instead, the stock will remain as one that belongs to a company with a small market cap, which offers unique opportunities to small investors when the stock is marked by a major news release.

This immunity to quoting delays however does not apply to other quote metrics such as the share price and the share volume, where a delay in the stream of data could swing an investor's decision undesirably in the wrong direction.

In this case, investors must have access to real-time price and volume data in order to formulate sound trading positions. These positions are based on the real-time share volume which defines the liquidity of the stock, and the real-time share price which defines the maximum number of shares that an investor can buy with a given capital. This data can be accessed freely on web pages providing up-to-the-minute price and volume updates such as in the illustrative example of real-time data shown in Figure 3.5.

Figure 3.5. Share price, share volume and percent change updated in real-time
(*Source:* www.nasdaq.com)

3-5.   OPEN-ACCESS INTRADAY AND EXTENDED WEB CHARTS

The Top Gainers List, along with quotes and real-time data, do not represent a sufficient pool of information that enables investors to frame sound trading positions on daily basis. To strengthen their trading positions, investors must also consider the stock charts which provide an intraday, as well as an extended history of the price and volume change for every stock trading publically on the floors of NYSE, NASDAQ and AMEX.

Similar to stock quotes, stock charts can be updated in real-time or can be delayed by 15 to 20 minutes depending upon the source. For extended charts which depict the price and volume change of the stock over a period exceeding one day (5 days and above such as the illustrative example shown in Figure 3.6), real-time updates are not possible. In fact, real-time updates are only applicable to intraday charts which represent the history of the price and volume change of a stock during every trading session.

In general, extended charts (5 days to 1 year in most cases) exhibit a significant influence on buying decisions as they enable investors to anticipate the projected impact of a news release on the performance of a stock in the session(s) following the news.

For instance, if a stock marked by a major news release has been losing value over the past three months as evidenced in the extended price chart, such stock will be poised to gain significantly more value as a consequence of the news release than a stock with similar quote metrics and the same news but which has been gaining value over the previous three months.

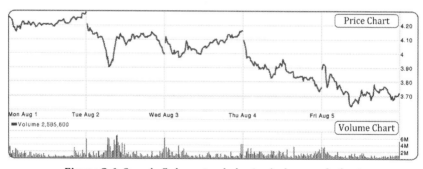

Figure 3.6. Sample 5-day extended price/volume web chart
(*Source:* finance.yahoo.com)

Such implications, in addition to the volatility rate of the stock and its ability to rally under a positive news outlook, can all be evidenced in the extended web chart which essentially portrays the record of the stock. For online investors relying on web resources for stock information, this record represents an essential tool that supplements the implications derived from the Top Gainers List and the quote metrics.

Therefore, online investors are encouraged to formulate their buying positions based on a combination of the Top Gainers List and extended charts, in order to draw an encompassing outline of a stock potential to rally on a positive news release before placing a buying order. Further discussions on the implications of extended web charts and their contribution to the formulation of trading positions will be outlined in Chapters 4 and 5.

Intraday web charts, on the other hand, differ from extended charts in that they visualize the variations in the price and volume of the stock during a single trading session, while extended charts visualize a broader history of the price and volume variations over a period exceeding five days. Depending upon the source, these extended charts may cover the whole trading history of the stock back to the initial public offering.

In general, intraday charts are more relevant to selling decisions, as opposed to extended charts which exhibit more influence on buying and holding decisions. A sample intraday chart showing price variations as a graph, and volume variations as a bar chart between 9:30 AM and 14:30 PM is presented in Figure 3.7.

Because intraday charts are more relevant to selling decisions, it is necessary to access such charts through a source that provides instantaneous updates, thus enabling investors to sell a stock before it drops *undesirably* in value. Online brokerage firms normally provide this service to their registered clientele. These intraday charts can also be found on open-access web pages (Figure 3.7) which provide a high level of update frequency, and therefore can be used to supplement the charting services provided by the broker.

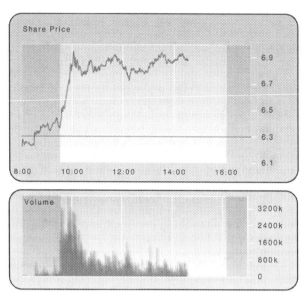

Figure 3.7. Sample intraday price (Top) and volume (Bottom) charts showing data between 9:30 AM and 14:30 PM (*Source:* www.nasdaq.com)

The level of details in the intraday chart may vary however from one source to the other. In some sources, the chart may be simplified with piecewise continuous straight lines that reduce the noisiness of the graph resulting from high trading activities on the stock. In other sources, the inherent noisiness of the price chart is maintained.

The difference between these two types of intraday chart visualization techniques is shown in Figure 3.8 for the same stock, where the original noisy chart is shown in Figure 3.8(A), and the corresponding simplified piecewise continuous chart is shown in Figure 3.8(B).

Although the two charts of Figure 3.8 reflect the performance of the same stock during the same intraday session, the difference in the level of details between the two charting sources is quite obvious. This difference is evidenced in many instances, such as the one at around 11:00 AM, where the spike labeled *L* on Figure 3.8(A) is completely filtered out on the equivalent simplified chart of Figure 3.8(B).

From an investor's perspective, the real-time noisy chart that visualizes all dips and spikes in the intraday price of a stock is more relevant to selling decisions than its simplified counterpart. In the piecewise continuous version of the chart, such sudden variations in the intraday share price are filtered or smoothed out, despite the fact that these behaviors significantly impact an investor's selling position, as they reveal the level of resistance that the stock is experiencing in real-time once it reaches a threshold price.

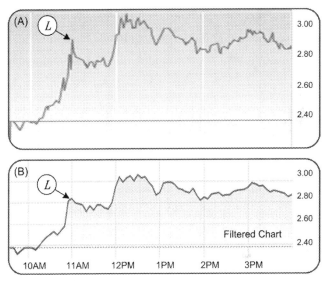

Figure 3.8. (A) Sample real-time chart for a given stock and (B) its equivalent piecewise continuous chart (*Source:* www.nasdaq.com & www.scottrade.com)

In the event where online investors do not have access to market models that attempt to predict the onset of resistance, real-time intraday noisy charts represent the only other alternative where resistance levels can be detected visually. Obviously, such visual detection requires a trial-and-error experience, but normally delivers consistency, provided that online investors employ instantaneous and noisy intraday charts as part of their trading strategy.

3-6. EXTENDED-HOURS QUOTES, CHARTS, AND TOP GAINERS LIST

In addition to intraday market quotes and charts, pre-market and after-hours data is also available on open-access web pages such as in the composite sample illustration shown in Figure 3.9. These quotes and charts are normally only pertinent to investors whose online accounts enable them to trade outside the regular market hours.

However, such data, especially pre-market data, also holds a considerable amount of information that enables investors trading during the regular hours to anticipate the intraday performance of the stock, and formulate their positions accordingly. Thus, it becomes necessary for online investors to incorporate extended hours quotes and charts in their market tools, and instate them as part of their regular trading methodologies.

Accessing such data is more difficult than regular-hours data, nonetheless. This is because many brokerage firms either limit their quoting and charting services to regular-hour trading, or offer extended hours charting services for only a few selected blue chip stocks.

However, such extended hours data can be found on open-access web pages for almost all companies that trade publically in the United States, either in the form of charts and quotes, or in the form of discrete-time data such as the samples shown in Figure 3.9. These services are also supplemented by extended-hours Top Gainers (Top Losers) Lists that rank the best (worst) performing stocks during the pre-market session, as well as during the after-hours session.

For investors placing orders at the beginning of the regular trading session, the pre-market Top Gainers List could represent a very useful tool, since it can provide an early insight into the selected stocks that may be poised for significant gains during the subsequent regular session based on recent press releases.

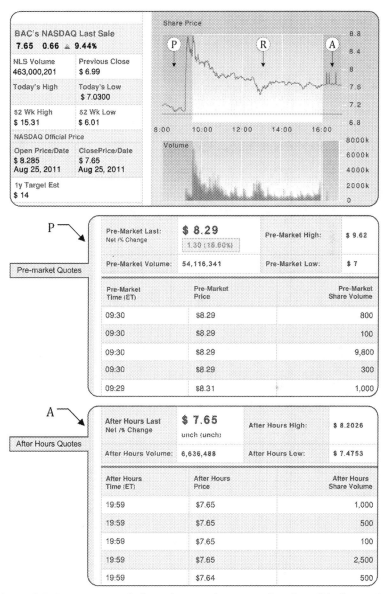

Figure 3.9. Composite stock chart showing the pre-market chart (P), the regular trading hours quotes and chart (R), the after-hour chart (A) and the corresponding pre-market and after-hour quotes (*Source:* www.nasdaq.com)

This insight allows investors to anticipate the listing of the regular-hours' Top Gainers List before it is updated, and ready themselves by analyzing the news releases and the quotes of the featured stocks prior to the opening of the regular intraday session.

3-7.   MARKET NEWS

Corporate news releases are simply the main driver of the stock market. Without news, the market remains sluggish, and opportunities to generate profit become very unlikely.

When a public company releases a corporate headline, the market reacts to the news one way or the other. If the news holds a positive prospect for the company, the stock will likely respond by gaining value to an extent that depends upon the connotations implied by the news. On the other hand, the stock will likely react by losing value if the news does not show any signs of a positive outlook.

In either case however, accessing such news as soon as it is released is very critical for investors. This is because instantaneous access to corporate news enables investors to formulate sound trading positions in a fast moving market; either by selling their positions and shorting the stock if the news is dismal, or by buying into the stock if the news reveals a promising outlook for profit.

For online investors, news releases are normally associated with every stock in a convenient way offered by the brokerage partner, or by open-access web pages such as in the sample shown in Figure 3.10. In particular, these open-access sources provide instantaneous updates of the headlines, in tandem with a corresponding update of the Top Gainers List (if applicable) throughout every trading session.

Last Trade:	3.25	Day's Range:	3.17 - 3.31	
Trade Time:	Aug 26	52wk Range:	2.98 - 6.45	
Change:	↑0.02 (0.62%)	Volume:	65,574,451	
Prev. Close:	3.23	Avg Vol (3m):	61,168,200	Quote
Open:	3.25	Market Cap	9.73B	
Bid:	3.24 x 4400	P/E (ttm)	N/A	
Ask:	3.26 x 10100	EPS (ttm):	-1.05	
1y Target Est:	5.75	Div & Yield:	N/A (N/A)	

Headlines

- A Fool Looks Back at Motley Fool (Sat 8.43AM EDT)
- The Motley Fool's Weekly Editor's Picks at Motley Fool (Sat 8:34AM EDT)
- Most Active New York Stock Exchange-traded stocks AP (Fri, Aug 26)
- FCC clock resumes on AT&T/T-Mobile deal review Reuters (Fri, Aug 26)
- Update: Clearwire Says It Hasn't Hired Restructuring Firm at Forbes (Fri, Aug 26)
- Clearwire May Be Contemplating Restructuring Its Debts at Motley Fool (Fri, Aug 26)
- Apple May End Mobile Phone Contract Era at Seeking Alpha (Fri, Aug
- Dish Plans Satellite-Terrestrial LTE Network at Forbes (Fri, Aug 26)
- UPDATE 1-FCC clock resumes on AT&T/T-Mobile deal review at Reuters (Fri, Aug 26)

News

Figure 3.10. Sample online quote for a selected stock with corresponding news releases sorted in a chronological order (*Source:* finance.yahoo.com)

These news releases (Figure 3.10) are further organized in a chronological order where they are sorted from the most recent to the least recent, allowing investors to quickly discern whether the movement of the stock is driven by news released on the same day of such movement, or whether the response of the stock is a reaction to earlier news releases. This chronological order saves online investors precious minutes when sorting through the Top Gainers List, especially in a fast moving market.

Chapter 4

INTERPRETING MARKET NEWS—PART I

4-1.   NEWS WITH MARKET CONNOTATIONS

Business news released by a public company reports the outcome of a corporate event, or informs shareholders and investors about new developments that affect the price of the company's public offering. Corporate news is generally released by companies themselves, or is written by an independent third party such as a research or advisory firm. Such events can range from the appointment of a new executive board, to delisting or bankruptcy filing.

Of all corporate news, those holding market connotations exhibit the most significant impact on the short-term reaction of the market to the company's stock offering. By definition, market connotations refer to a set of developments whose outcome impacts the broader consumer market in the form of commodities or consumer products.

The potential of a corporate activity to exhibit a positive impact on a consumer market makes the company's public offering very attractive to investors. This is because the consumer market offers public firms considerable opportunities for growth, which increases their profit and ultimately their dividend yield.

With the prospects of increased dividends, shareholders react to corporate news with market connotations by either holding or buying more shares in the company's public offering. This action automatically drives the share price up where the upward trend may, not only be noticeable in the immediate trading session following the press release, but also over an extended period of time depending upon the significance of such connotations.

For corporations with a small market cap, the influx of investors and shareholders' money creates an unusual trading volume. This high volume activity, coupled with positive market connotations, enables the stock of such companies to gain an unusual momentum that may double, or even triple the share price in the immediate session following the press release.

Because such market reactions are news-dependent, they can seldom be predicted by quantitative models. In fact, the only guaranteed approach for taking advantage of these opportunities is through a fundamental understanding of the market dynamics, and a thorough interpretation of corporate news on daily basis. This interpretation is one of the key elements that enable investors to formulate sound trading positions based on factual data, more so than speculations where the trading strategies are founded on hopes and expectations.

The focus of this chapter is therefore on streamlining such interpretations and associating them with market analyses (quotes and charts) discussed in the previous chapters. This process is further supported by real examples of business news with market connotations, and is supplemented by a factual visualization of the impact such news exhibits on the immediate behavior of the stock in the trading session(s) following the release.

Nonetheless, the readers are advised to note that the examples addressed in this chapter are not exclusive. This means that their use is for illustration purposes and not for biased selectivity, where it may be erroneously hinted that only those sectors featured in this chapter hold the potential for exhibiting market connotations.

In reality, because of recurrent market trends, any press release that shares common attributes with the examples presented in this chapter can be considered as holding market connotations, and therefore should be analyzed diligently for profit prospects.

4-2.   ENERGY SECTOR

An example that reflects an energy-related press release with market connotations refers to a company engaged in the exploration and production of oil and natural gas. This US-based company operates two wells in an offshore site for which an independent study was carried out to estimate the total recoverable in-place resources.

An excerpt from the actual news release reads as follows: "... *the report concludes that the best estimate for undiscovered original oil-in-place is 1.9 billion barrels, with a high of 6.3 billion barrels; and the best estimate for associated recoverable and un-risked prospective oil resources is 626 million barrels with a high of 2.2 billion barrels. This is significantly higher than the estimated 500 million barrels of potential recoverable oil detailed in the Company's recent investor presentation . . ." (Source: Business wire).*

An investor reading this news release after spotting the company's stock on the Top Gainers List (for instance) should interpret the news as follows: The original oil reserves that the company expected to recover from its operations on the offshore well are 20% less than the actual recoverable oil, with the potential of extracting almost four times as much oil as was originally anticipated.

Since oil is a precious commodity sought by every consumer on a global scale, the possibility of extracting and selling four times more oil than initially anticipated means that the company will potentially be capable of deriving more profit from its operations over a longer period of time.

These are the market connotations that this news report exhibits in its content, which are significant enough to draw an unusual volume activity on the stock in the immediate session following the release. This is evidenced in Figure 4.1, where the stock gained a maximum of 61% in intraday share value before closing the session at 43%.

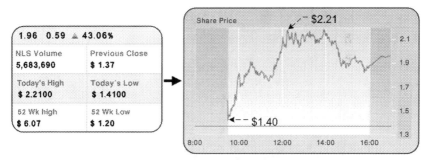

Figure 4.1. Intraday chart showing the rise in the share price of an Energy stock as a consequence of a news release holding market connotations
(*Source:* www.nasdaq.com)

However, for a small investor seeking to maximize profit on short-term basis, this news alone may not be enough to formulate a sound buying position. In fact, if this news report relates to a company whose share price is expensive (above $10), or to a company whose extended price chart shows an upward trend for the past 3 to 6 months (for instance), this news release may not impact the share price to the extent it did with the stock shown in Figure 4.1.

In the case of this example, a closer look at the quotes and extended charts of this company reveals that the stock's 52-Week range is

$1.20-$6.07, and that the stock had been losing value over the previous six months.

This leads to the conclusion that the stock is very likely undervalued as it is trading at the lower bounds of its 52-week range, which further strengthens the likelihwood of a significant price spike, and solidifies the soundness of a buying order placed at the opening of the trading session.

Another example with similar market connotations relating to the energy sector refers to a company with a news release that reads as follows: *". . . the independent oil and gas company announced the completion of its horizontal well. The well is expected to be put on production in a few weeks and the company expects it to meet or exceed expectations of 500 barrels of oil per day. That will increase its net production, cash flow and net produced reserves significantly, the company said . . ." (Source: The Street Journal).*

The completion of a horizontal well in itself is an achievement for this small-cap company due to the challenges associated with horizontal drilling as opposed to more traditional vertical drilling. This in general strengthens the corporate credibility of the company, while concurrently enabling it to extract more oil than would have otherwise been possible without horizontal drilling.

This piece of the news report alone is significant enough to cause the stock price to gain a measurable value over more than one consecutive trading session. The extended trend in this case will be sustained by this reported accomplishment which supplements the market connotations and strengthens the overall credibility of the company's operations.

More important however are the market connotations this news report exhibits in its content. The ability to extract more oil because of horizontal drilling signifies that the company will be capable of selling more of the well-sought-after commodity of oil. This will subsequently increase its revenues and profit as a consequence of this accomplishment.

On short-term basis, a buying position founded on these connotations is further strengthened by the fact that the company's price at the time of the press release was $2.03, which falls around the middle range of the 52-Week price of $0.76-$3.10. Moreover, the company's market cap is only $35 million, with an extended price chart (Figure 4.2) that shows the stock price relatively stagnant (and on decline) for the previous four months.

These three factors together, combined with the market connotations that the press release holds in its content, prove that the stock has the potential to increase in value significantly, driven by an unusual interest in the company's performance (Figure 4.2).

Figure 4.2. Extended chart showing an 84% increase in an Energy stock price on an unusual volume following a news release with market connotations (*Source:* finance.yahoo.com)

This unusual volume caused the stock to gain 84% in value in the immediate reaction to the news release as shown in the extended chart of Figure 4.2. It further enabled the share price to continue its upward trend subsequently to achieve a peak percent gain of 144% (from $2.03 to $4.95) at the end of the fourth trading session.

4-3. PHARMACEUTICAL SECTOR

The market connotations exhibited by corporate news released by pharmaceutical companies often relate to the completion of a pivotal study with significant results, or to the approval of a new treatment or drug for the consumer market.

An example of a press release detailing the progress of a pivotal study refers to a company that engages in innovative research in biotechnology for therapy in diabetes and metabolic syndrome. An excerpt from the news release reads: *"... (Company X) today announced that its drug candidate achieved statistically significant reductions in cholesterol . . . . for nine weeks to genetically engineered mice prone to Dyslipidemia. The aortas of these mice also showed reductions in the extent of atherosclerotic lesions as measured by lesion area in response to treatment. These analysis and lesion measurement results represent the final data from the study . . . ."* (*Source: PR Newswire*).

The connotations exhibited by this news release are important, not only because of the considerable statistical results that this study has established, but also because the company will not be investing any additional resources on research and development as those results represent the final data of the study. This strengthens the scientific legitimacy of these results and moves the company one step closer towards commercializing the ensuing product.

Furthermore, because the study targets high-cholesterol, which is a disease that affects a large portion of the global population, the possibility of turning those *final* research results into a drug or a treatment will provide the opportunity to target a large commercial market on the global scale. This will potentially enable the company to increase its profit and subsequently its dividends on the long-term.

These are the market connotations that can be synthesized from this press release, which are very significant to cause an unusual interest in the stock as evidenced in the intraday chart shown in Figure 4.3. This chart represents the reaction of the market in the immediate session following the press release.

From a short-term trading perspective, the analysis of the stock's quotes and extended charts further solidify the soundness of a buying position formulated at the beginning of the trading session shown in Figure 4.3. In fact, the quotes of this stock show a 52-Week price range of $1.23-$21.0, with a market cap of around $3 million. This means that the company releasing this news is a small corporation with a stock trading at the lower bound of the 52-week range, where the opening price for the intraday session of Figure 4.3 was $1.35. Furthermore, the extended three-month chart of the stock reveals a steady decline in the share price from $3.5 down to $1.35 as reflected in Figure 4.4.

Figure 4.3. Intraday chart showing a pharmaceutical stock rallying on a press release holding market connotations pertaining to the completion of the final stages of a pivotal medical study (*Source:* www.nasdaq.com)

All these facts imply that the company is largely undervalued. This undervaluation, combined with the positive prospects for market growth as reflected in the press release, constitute a major incentive for an unusual investors' interest in the stock.

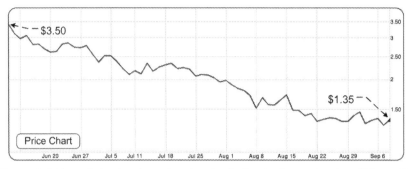

Figure 4.4. Extended price chart showing the decline in the stock price of Figure 4.3 over a period of three months prior to the release of a corporate news with market connotations (*Source:* finance.yahoo.com)

This influx of investors' money on an unusual volume (the average three-month volume of the stock is 16,000 shares compared to a volume of more than one million shares during the session following the press release) generated an increase in the share price by about 155% in the first 45 minutes of trading (Figure 4.3), before losing momentum and closing the session at 96%.

An interesting aspect of this example is the fact that this significant increase in the share price occurred on a day when the Dow Jones Industrial Average lost 2.69% in value. This falls in line with the recommendations made earlier in Chapter 1, where individual investors were advised not to rely on market indices to formulate their trading positions, as such indices tend to overshadow the positive movement of smaller corporations. In fact, as evidenced in Figure 4.3, small-cap stocks always present ample opportunities for small investors to derive short-term profit, even during trading sessions marked by a decline in the major indices.

A second example of a pharmaceutical stock rallying on a press release with market connotations relates to the approval of a new treatment developed by a biotechnology company for commercial practice in a big market.

An excerpt from the company's news release reads as follows: *". . . (Company X) has gained certification of its laboratory under the US Clinical Laboratories Improvements Amendments . . . . This certification is the culmination of preparations required for the US launch of the . . . breast cancer test . . . which is a test that informs clinicians about their patients' individual, non-familial, sporadic risk of breast cancer. This product fulfills an unmet need by better classifying women at moderate risk of breast cancer who would potentially benefit from preventive therapy . . . . This is the first test of its kind to give women a cost effective personal assessment of their individual risk of breast cancer . . ."* (*Source: PR Newswire*).

Unlike the first pharmaceutical example, the market connotations included in this press release are explicit in this case, where the company publically announces the completion of the first step towards the release of its new product into the American market.

However, the more interesting aspect of this technology is that it can be used for the *personal* assessment of individual risk. This means that the product use is not only restricted to medical centers and physicians, but rather broadened to the larger consumer market where individuals can utilize it to assess their exposure to the risk on the personal level.

The broader application of this new technology offers the company the opportunity to tap into an even larger market, which will increase its revenues and profits. Such connotation is significant enough to enable the company's stocks to gain value in the immediate investors' reaction to this news release, as well as over an extended period as shown in the price chart depicted in Figure 4.5.

However, as with all the other examples presented in this chapter, a buying position formulated on these market connotations must be further strengthened by an analysis of the quotes and extended price charts of the stock. Such analysis reveals that the company's market cap is $107 million with an average volume of 215,000 shares.

Figure 4.5. Extended price and volume chart showing the increase in share price on an unusual volume after the release of news reporting the launch of a new consumer product (*Source:* finance.yahoo.com)

This means that the company is financially stable and is not characterized by a high volatility rate since its average daily volume is reasonably high. This position generally entices investors to hold their stakes and generates an extended interest in the stock offering as a reaction to this press release. Such hold/buy positions can be further encouraged by the fact that the 52-Week range of the stock is $0.65-$9.24, which puts the share price at the lower bounds of this range at the time of the news release.

All these factors combined, prove that this stock has a great potential to increase in value over an extended period of time (Figure 4.5), where the share price gained 72% in the immediate session following the news release, and a total of 152% over a period of five consecutive trading sessions (from $3.17/share to $8.00/share).

4-4.   CONSUMER ELECTRONICS SECTOR

The consumer electronics sector represents an ever growing market that attracts a considerable attention from investors when a news report holding market connotations is released.

One of the examples that illustrate this interest refers to a manufacturer of a high-performance memory systems whose news report reads as follows: ". . . (Company X) is demonstrating the world's first 16GB virtual rank double-data-rate three, registered dual in-line memory module . . . . This demonstration reinforces (the module's) ability to function as a standard RDIMM while increasing memory bandwidth and capacity for datacenter servers. The technology on HP industry-standard servers increases server memory capacity and bandwidth to enhance application performance in converged infrastructures . . . (Company X) plans to sample (the memory module) to major OEM customers in December with production slated for (the next quarter) . . ." (Source: PRNewswire).

Interpreting the market connotations exhibited by this news report is straightforward: A technology company has released a new electronic product that increases the performance of data servers and is compatible with HP's existing servers.

Because HP is a major manufacturer of computer products, the compatibility of this new technology with existing HP products means that this small-cap company will be able to integrate its memory module directly into an existing large market.

This will be further enhanced by the company's intentions to cooperate with other major customers, and by the plan to start production in the upcoming few months following this press release. This plan reinforces the final stages of development of the technology and solidifies the credibility of the product and its marketability.

These long-term objectives, coupled with the immediate collaboration with a major computer manufacturer, are significant to cause an extended interest in the company's stock offering (Figure 4.6). Such interest is sustained by the commercial aspect of this product and the increased impact it will have on the company's dividend yield.

The extended reaction to these connotations is visualized in Figure 4.6, where the stock price gained 50% in the immediate reaction to the news, and continued the upward climb in the following six days, generating a cumulative increase of 600% in share value (from $0.89 to $6.24).

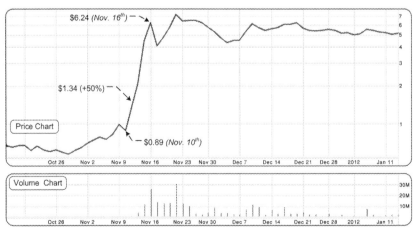

Figure 4.6. Price and volume chart showing the increase in investors' interest in a consumer electronic stock following the release of a new marketable product (*Source:* finance.yahoo.com)

Another example of the consumer electronics sector that shares common attributes with the first one is used to illustrate the recurrent aspect of market connotations. This is evidenced in a press report released by a developer of hardware and software technology that enables secure access to digital content in computers and flash drives.

An excerpt from this press release reads: *". . . (Company X) announced earlier this morning that its technology has been selected as the exclusive supplier of near-field . . . RFID stickers for the roll out of Google's marketing campaign. . . . Google is currently testing the service in Austin (Texas), distributing the stickers to local business owners to help connect them to consumers and advertize their products and services . . ."*

Despite the fact that this press release outlines the integration of the referenced RFID product into a very specific market (Austin, Texas), the selection of this technology by *Google*, which is a large corporation and a leader in Internet services, could pave the path for future collaboration and market expansion for this medium-cap company ($\sim$ \$150 million). However, such possibilities or intentions have not been explicitly outlined in this press release, which undermines its long-term market connotations.

Nonetheless, this fact does not prevent the stock from gaining significant value in the immediate market reaction, based on the possibility of further expansion and the factual existing collaboration with *Google*. Such reaction is depicted in Figure 4.7, which shows an 87% increase in intraday share value driven by an unusual volume (the average three-month volume prior to this press release is 77,000 shares).

However, from a short-term investment perspective, holding this stock for more than one session may be very risky as the connotations do not carry any explicit indications of future expansion. This makes the stock more prone to losing its unusual momentum in the subsequent session(s) following the press release.

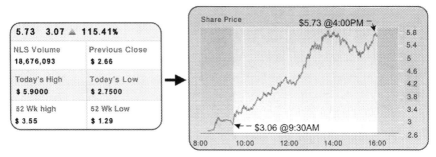

Figure 4.7. Price chart showing the intraday reaction of the market to a press release outlining the collaboration of a medium-cap corporation with *Google* (*Source:* www.nasdaq.com)

4-5. COMMUNICATION SECTOR

Similar to all the other industries presented earlier in this chapter, the communication sector represents a vast market which draws a significant interest from investors when corporate news holding market connotations pertinent to this sector is released.

The significance of such press reports is illustrated in the following sample excerpt: *". . . (Company X) announced that its semiconductor technology has been officially approved by China's Ministry of Industry and Information Technology (MIIT), a government entity responsible for the regulation and development of China's wireless industry. The approval signifies that . . . the technology is qualified for use in LTE networks in China. (Company X) semiconductor solution has been undergoing testing for several months while interoperating with leading system vendors Huawei, and Alcatel-Lucent Shanghai Bell . . . . The successful passing of the tests indicates that (Company*

X's) technology supports the MIIT performance and interoperability requirements necessary for the technology to be used in the field . . ." (Source: Business Wire).

Because China represents a large consumer market for mobile communication, the approval of this semiconductor technology to be used in mobile devices in the Chinese market means that the company's prospects for increasing its profits are substantial.

Such prospects are even further strengthened by the partnership that the company has already established with leading system vendors in the Chinese market, and by the successful completion of initial tests carried in collaboration with these major vendors. These three combined accomplishments reinforce the ability of this medium-cap company to tap into the vast consumer resources of the Chinese market, and increase its revenues and dividend yield.

These are the market connotations exhibited in this press release, which are very substantial to draw an unusual volume in the immediate session following the news as shown in the extended chart of Figure 4.8.

The ability of the stock to rally as a consequence of these connotations is further sustained by the fact that the stock price had been losing value in the three-month period prior to this press release. This means that the stock is likely undervalued, where its price ($4.43/share) falls at the lower bounds of the 52-Week range of $4.23-$19.5.

This likelihood of undervaluation, coupled with the market connotations exhibited in the press release, enabled the stock to gain 92% in intraday value before closing the session at 68% (Figure 4.8).

Figure 4.8. Extended 5-day price and volume chart showing a decline in share value, followed by an unusual spike subsequent to the release of a news holding market connotations pertinent to the communication sector (*Source:* finance.yahoo.com)

4-6.   OUTTAKE

This chapter focused on the interpretation of market connotations exhibited by corporate press releases. The recurrent impact of these connotations on the short-term performance of a given stock was visualized through multiple factual examples. These examples highlighted the ability of a stock to gain a substantial value in the immediate reaction to such news, as well during the subsequent sessions following the press release (when applicable).

Therefore, the objective of this chapter was to highlight the recurrent reaction of the market to such corporate news that exhibits market connotations in its content. Because of this recurrent nature, investors that can recognize these patterns and decipher these connotations are likely capable of generating significant profits on short-term basis.

One aspect to note in this process is that corporate news with market connotations is very often released. This makes the fundamental understanding of these patterns and the ability to interpret this type of news worthwhile, since such skill enables investors to formulate sound profitable buying positions based on facts interpretation rather than speculations.

In this direction, the examples presented in this chapter should represent the basis for these interpretations, where individual investors can extrapolate this analysis to similar corporate news pertinent to any other sector of the broader stock market.

Chapter 5

INTERPRETING MARKET NEWS—PART II

5-1. NEWS WITH NO MARKET CONNOTATIONS

The focus of the previous chapter was on the interpretation of corporate news for market connotations that generate an unusual volume reaction on the stock market. The discussion further highlighted—through factual examples—the ability of these connotations to deliver a triple digit percent increase in the stock price in the immediate reaction of the market to such news.

In the current chapter, the discussion focuses on the interpretation of corporate press releases that can generate a measurable increase in the stock price, without necessarily carrying direct market connotations in their content. This type of news is very commonly released on the stock market, as it encompasses a wide range of corporate activities ranging from the appointment of a board member, to delisting notices and bankruptcy.

Unlike corporate news with market connotations whose positive impact on the stock's momentum is largely predictable, the influence of news releases that carry no market connotations is relatively more difficult to predict. This is because the market reaction to this news is not explicitly sustained by an unequivocal event that ties the stock performance to prospective market growth. Instead, corporate news with no market connotations often entices speculations with respect to its impact on the long-term performance of the stock. These speculations make the anticipation of the stock direction in reaction to the news release less consistent.

To concretize this difference between the two aforementioned types of corporate news, consider a press release that reports on a company's approval of its product for a new commercial market (for instance, the Asian market), compared to another press release that reports an event where a company's chief-executive is presenting a new product at a corporate conference.

In the first news report, the explicit market connotations unequivocally inform investors about the expansion of the company's business into a new market, which raises the prospects of profit and increases the dividend yield. In the second report, there are no such explicit connotations. The fact that a new product is presented at a conference does not necessarily mean that the product carries a real market value. This leaves investors' speculating about the significance of the press release, which normally lessens the upward momentum of the stock in the immediate reaction to the news.

Nonetheless, because of the plethora of corporate news that carries no market connotations, it becomes important to highlight the recurrent impact that some of these most frequent press releases exhibit on the performance of the stock. The examples discussed in this chapter represent a sample of such news reports that typically generate a *consistent* upward momentum on the stock, and should be used as a basis for interpreting any other similar corporate news that holds no market connotations.

5-2. EARNINGS REPORT

Earnings reports are the most common corporate news released on the stock market. Every public company issues at least one such report at the end of every quarter outlining the results of its operations during this period. Thus, learning how to interpret earnings reports is a critical factor for the formulation of trading positions, as the connotations they carry are largely recurrent.

Earnings reports can be broadly classified into three categories. One category refers to financial statements that outline an exceptional performance of the company's operations. A second category refers to reports that achieve better-than-expected encouraging results, and a third category that achieves modest positive results.

Although earnings reports can also outline negative results from a company's quarterly operations, such reports will not be considered in this discussion as they generally create a negative momentum on the stock, and thus should be avoided by short-term investors.

5-2-1. Exceptional Earnings Reports

An exceptional earnings report is one that outlines a significant triple-digit percent increase in a company's profit, or a significant dividend distribution to investors. An excerpt from one such report reads as follows: *"... The Company achieved income from operations in the period of $342,000. However, mainly due to a non-cash reversal of allowance for bad debt generating other income of $32,022,000 in the quarter, the Company reported net income of $32.03 million or $12.73 per share, compared with a loss of $(446,000) or $(0.18) per share a year earlier..." (Source: MarketWire).*

An EPS (Earnings per Share) of $12.73 is exceptionally high. This is made even more outstanding by the fact that the current positive EPS compares to a negative EPS of $0.18 resulting from the non-profitable operations carried over the previous year. Such data in and of itself is very significant to cause an immediate rally on the stock as exhibited in Figure 5.1.

Figure 5.1. Intraday price chart showing the reaction of the market to an earnings report with an exceptional dividend distribution (*Source:* www.nasdaq.com)

Exceptional earnings reports such as these represent a solid opportunity for profit on short-term basis. However, buying positions formulated on these reports should also be strengthened by analyzing the quotes of the stock. In the case of the example shown in Figure 5.1, the company has a small market cap of $3 million, and a 52-week range of $0.6-$4.88, which places the opening price of $1.01 on the day of this press release at the lower bounds of this range.

With a share price that is largely undervalued, and an extended price chart showing a price decline in the previous month, the exceptional EPS rate caused the stock to spike on an unusual volume in the immediate reaction to the press release. This volume enabled the stock to gain 172% in intraday value (from $1.09 to $2.97), before closing the trading session at 123% ($2.44/share).

5-2-2. Encouraging Earnings Reports

Financial statements that don't report an outstanding performance of a public company, but provide positive data that shows encouraging signs of progress also generate an unusual interest in the stock. The extent by which such interest impacts the stock price will likely be inferior to that exhibited in reaction to exceptional earnings reports. Nonetheless, positive encouraging performances are always welcome news on the market, drawing considerable attention from short-term investors.

To illustrate such reaction through an example, consider the following excerpt from a biotechnology company whose 5-day price and volume charts are shown in Figure 5.2: "*. . . Revenue was $439.3 million, an increase of $104.2 million or 31.1% compared to prior year . . . Net income was $2.9 million or $0.05 per diluted share, compared to prior year net loss of $7.2 million, or $0.18 per share . . ." (Source: Business wire).*

An increase of 31.1% in annual revenues is substantial, especially when the net profit derived from these revenues earned shareholders a positive EPS of $0.05/share, which compares to a negative EPS over the previous year where shareholders incurred a net loss of $0.18/share.

The performance difference between the current and previous example is obvious from the stand-point of earnings and dividend distribution. This is further reflected in the market reaction to the news, where in the example of Figure 5.2, the stock achieved a peak intraday price gain of 37% for an EPS of $0.18/ share, compared to a peak intraday of 172% for the example of Figure 5.1 with an EPS of $12.73/ share.

Figure 5.2. A 5-day price and volume chart showing investors' reaction to an earnings report with encouraging data reflecting positive annual operations (*Source:* finance.yahoo.com)

5-2-3. Modest Earnings Reports

A modest earnings report is one that outlines a moderately significant increase in revenues and profits, to an extent that it does not create an unusual influx of short-term investors on the stock in the immediate reaction to the news.

An excerpt from a sample of such reports reads: ". . . *Revenues increased modestly to $8.3 million from $8.2 million . . . Operating income increased to $0.8 million from breakeven operating results in the (previous) quarter, while gross margin increased by 2.3% . . . Net income totaled $5.9 million, or $0.20 per diluted share, compared to a net loss of $0.2 million, or $0.01 per diluted share in the same period last year . . .*" (*Source: PR Newswire*).

The modest increase in the revenues outlined in this report will typically exhibit an insignificant positive influence on the short-term price of the stock. In fact, if the current EPS did not increase relative to the EPS of the previous year (likely due to reduction in operating cost), the market will most certainly show little interest in this news in the immediate reaction after its release. However, because of this positive EPS, a modest increase of 16% in intraday share value was noted—as reflected in Figure 5.3—before the stock ended the session at 11%.

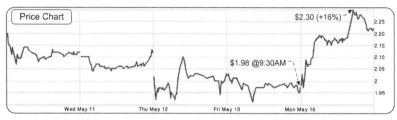

Figure 5.3. A 5-day extended price chart showing a 16% spike in the share price of a stock in reaction to a modest earnings report (*Source:* finance.yahoo.com)

Nonetheless, despite this positive increase in share value, short-term traders should note that investors' reaction to such modest earnings reports tends to be influenced by the overall direction of the market. In fact, the positive momentum depicted in Figure 5.4 in the trading session following the press release would likely be less significant if the press release coincided with a trading session marked by a negative trend in the major indices.

5-3.   MERGER AND ACQUISITION

A *merger* refers to a corporate action where two companies consent on combining assets to create a new larger firm. Often times, a merger involves the consolidation of two firms of the same market size. An *acquisition* on the other hand denotes a corporate action where a large firm purchases the assets of a smaller firm and annexes them to its business portfolio.

In a merger transaction, the consolidation of two firms carries long-term connotations which are reflected in the financial security that a merger furnishes to the firm's business and shareholders. In an acquisition transaction, the connotations are more transitory, and are depicted in the higher bid price that the acquiring firm often offers for the common shares of the acquired firm in order to entice shareholders to sell their stakes.

From a trading perspective, the long-term connotations exhibited in a merger action tend to create an extended positive momentum on the stock price. This is in contrast to an acquisition action whose short-term connotations most notably impact the stock price in the immediate session following the news.

An illustration of the market reaction to merger-related news refers to the following excerpt from a press release: "... (Company X and Company Y) today announced plans to merge ... The merger of these 100-year-old institutions will create a ... community banking organization with approximately $2.9 billion in assets, $2.4 billion in deposits and 63 full-service banking offices located in some of the state's most robust markets ... As part of this transaction ... two private equity firms with a history of successful investing in the financial services sector, have each entered into definitive agreements ... to invest $77.5 million in the common stock of (the merged companies), subject to the conditions set forth in the agreements as part of a $310 million private placement ..." (Source: Marketwire).

The two companies merging in this news are small-cap banking firms whose stocks are trading under $1/share. This means that the merging action is most likely motivated by the risk of delisting, and is therefore tailored towards increasing the companies' capital to avert such risk, and furnish shareholders with the financial security to hold their stakes.

More significant however are the investments that two private equity firms committed to the merged corporations. This private placement solidifies the grounds of the merger, where the investment action is seen as favoring the transaction and supporting the credibility of the merger.

The combination of these two corporate actions reported in the press release (the merger and the private equity placement) is substantially significant to cause the stock to rally over an extended period following the news report. This momentum is shown in Figure 5.4, where the stock price gained value over a consecutive 5-day period.

The price hike exhibited in Figure 5.4 in reaction to the merger report is further sustained by the undervalued position of the stock at the time of the report. In fact, the stock quotes on the day of the news release show a 52-Week range of $0.44-$1.89. This places the opening price of $0.54 at the lower bound of the price range.

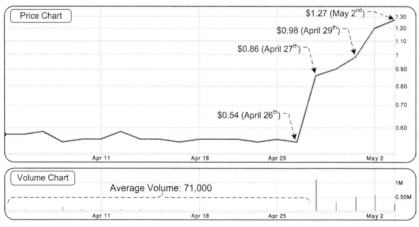

Figure 5.4. A one-month price and volume chart showing the extended reaction of the market to a merger press release (*Source:* finance.yahoo.com)

Furthermore, the extended price chart of the stock shows a decline in the share price over the previous five months. This position, combined with the undervaluation of the stock and the merger and private placement transactions, caused the stock to gain 60% in value in the immediate session following the report, and a total of 135% ($0.54 to $1.27) over a consecutive period of five sessions.

5-4.   SECURING A CONTRACT

When a public company secures a new contract, the news normally draws a short-term interest in the stock that largely depends on the value of the contract, weighted against the size and market cap of the company. For instance, a firm with a $5 million market cap awarded a $1 million contract is more likely to rally on the news than a company with a $100 million market cap awarded the same contract.

To illustrate this process through an example, consider the following excerpt from a press release that reads as follows: *". . . (Company X), a provider of customized heavy duty lifting and carrying machinery, today announced it has signed a new equipment contract for a marine hoist . . . A Chinese government control center signed a contract with (Company X) for approximately $400,000 to purchase a 50 ton marine hoist. This represents the second industry that (Company X) has been able to penetrate with its customized marine hoist and is a large market that can lead to future sales . . ."* *(Source: PR Newswire).*

This $400,000 contract constitutes almost 15% of the firm's $6 million market cap. While this represents a substantially lucrative opportunity for the company, the significance of the news is further exhibited in the statement that points to the large market that this company has managed to penetrate with this contract, and to the prospects of increased future sales.

If this contract was awarded to a larger company (for instance, with a $50 million market cap), the impact of this news on the short-term momentum of the stock will likely be less significant. However, because of the small market cap of this firm and the market connotations that hint to the prospects of increased future sales, the reaction of the market to this news is more compelling. This is further sustained by the declining stock price during the previous six months (Figure 5.5), and by the undervalued position of the stock whose opening price ($1.30) at the time of the press release fell at the lower bounds of the 52-Week range.

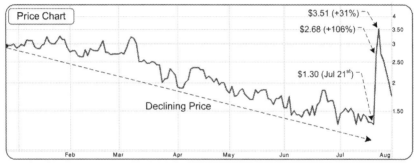

Figure 5.5. Extended chart showing a continual decline in the share price prior to a 170% price hike in reaction to a market news outlining the details of a new contract awarded to a small-cap firm (*Source:* finance.yahoo.com)

All these factors combined, caused the stock to rally over two consecutive trading sessions, gaining 106% in the first session following the news, and an additional 31% in the second session for a total price gain of 170% (from $1.30 to $ 3.51) as shown in Figure 5.5.

However, despite the ability of a news report that outlines the details of a newly awarded contract to cause a spike in the share price, such spike is normally short-lived. Investors are therefore advised not hold these stocks for more than one trading session, since the unusual momentum will likely retreat considerably in the following sessions as reflected in Figure 5.5 after the price peaked at $3.51.

5-5.   DELISTING NOTICE

One of the most controversial news contents that tend to create a positive momentum on the stock is a delisting notice. A public company receives this notice if its stocks traded under $1/share for more than one month. When this happens, the company has a limited time to regain compliance and avoid delisting.

Ironically however, despite the negative connotations carried by a delisting notice, the news itself often generates a positive momentum on the stock as shareholders try to avoid delisting by driving the share price up towards the bounds of the $1 range. This momentum is typically short-lived, but the reaction of the market to the delisting notice is sometimes very significant that adventurous investors may be enticed to ride the upward momentum for short-term profits.

An example of such news reads as follows: *"... (Company X) received a notice from NASDAQ ... that for the last 30 consecutive business days the bid price for the Company's common stock had closed below the minimum $1.00 per share ... The notification letter states that the Company will have 180 calendar days ... to regain compliance .... In order to regain compliance, shares of the Company's common stock must maintain a minimum bid closing price of at least $1.00 per share for a minimum of ten consecutive business days ..."* (*Source: EdgarOnline*).

This news is classically recurrent for delisting notices. In the case of the quoted example, the immediate market reaction generated a 25% increase in the stock price. Typically however, the extent by which this news impacts the stock price is random and difficult to predict.

Therefore, in order to minimize the risk of exposure, short-term investors are recommended to analyze the extended price chart for declining patterns before formulating a buying position on stocks driven by delisting notices.

5-6. OUTTAKE

Corporate press releases that don't contain implicit or explicit market connotations can also exhibit a significant impact on the momentum of the stock in the immediate reaction following the news. This reaction is often short-lived, but could cause a considerable hike in the stock price when the appropriate driving circumstances are furnished.

The examples discussed in this chapter represent a sample of such corporate news that exhibits consistent market reaction when the stock quotes show signs of undervaluation. These examples are meant to serve as a basis for this interpretation, despite the recognized difficulty in anticipating the stock reaction to corporate news that shows no direct indication of market connotations.

Nonetheless, the examples presented in this chapter are quite recurrent, and their impact on the stock momentum is predictable. This means that short-term investors can scout the market (and the Top Gainers List) for this news, and benefit from the upward price trend when such momentum is supported by appropriate undervalued quotes.

Selling these stocks is nonetheless recommended during the same intraday session as this upward price trend is prone to losing momentum in subsequent sessions, ultimately wiping out the short-term gains.

Chapter 6

CORPORATE NEWS TO AVOID

In the previous two chapters, the discussion focused on the press releases that generate a significant short-term increase in the stock price when coupled with a quote analysis showing signs of undervaluation. These press releases were separated into two categories. One category that aggregates news carrying market connotations, and another category that aggregates news with no market connotations but which exhibits recurrent (considerable) positive trends on the stock price.

In the current chapter, the focus is on the remaining press releases which can be clustered into a third class that is unrelated to the two previously established categories. This class is delineated in the context of this chapter as the "No Big Deals" press releases, where the news carries no major connotations with respect to the current or prospective business outlook and growth potential of a public company. This type of news, although carrying positive data, rarely generates a significant increase in the stock price, and thus should be avoided by short-term small investors.

A collection of examples depicting this class of news is presented in this chapter, along with factual press excerpts and price and volume charts that visualize the modest short-term reaction of the market to the "No Big Deals"—type of news.

6-1.   LIMITED SALE TRANSACTION

A limited sale transaction refers to a press release that delineates the sale of a specific product to a specific customer, without explicitly outlining any details about the impact of this transaction on the company's market growth and prospective business opportunities.

An example of such news is illustrated in the following excerpt:

"... *(Company X) announced it has sold an ... MRI (machine) to a physician practice of radiologists and neurosurgeons. The MRI will be placed in a newly-constructed 50,000 sq. ft. building, increasing the practice to 75,000 sq. ft. for the new state-of-the-art neuroscience spine institute ... The group who purchased the ... MRI, said they wanted the best diagnostic device ... Accordingly, they considered other state-of-the-art MRI scanners ... but those systems are single-position only and non-weight bearing. They therefore concluded that to be a "Center of Excellence for the Spine," it was crucial to have an MRI that could evaluate the spine in its full range of dynamic weight-bearing positions ..."* (*Source: MarketWire*).

The "No Big Deals" connotations carried by this news are obvious. The sale of a single quantity of the company's product to a specific customer does not hint to any substantial forthcoming business opportunities. Even though the news carries positive information, the long-term connotations of the transaction are—to a large extent—insignificant since they reflect no prospective market growth as a result of this deal.

The reaction of the market to this type of news is not surprisingly modest. This is reflected in Figure 6.1 for the selected example which shows the intraday price chart in the immediate market reaction to the quoted press release.

Despite the short early morning ascent in Figure 6.1, the stock price quickly lost momentum and closed the session up by only 7%. In fact, a day-trader acquiring a stake at 9:30 AM at $2.37/share and holding it for more than 15 minutes would have incurred a loss as a result of this buying position and the declining intraday momentum.

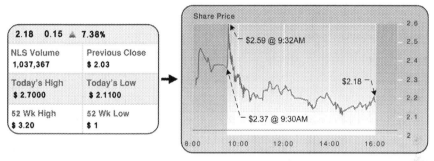

Figure 6.1. Intraday price chart showing the reaction of the market to a limited sale transaction (*Source:* www.nasdaq.com)

From a short-term trading perspective, small investors are recommended to avoid trading with stocks marked by a press release delineating limited sale transaction news. This recommendation becomes more compelling when the news reflects no explicit evidence about the projected impact of this transaction on the long-term growth prospects of the company.

6-2. CONFERENCE PRESENTATION

Another class of news that short-term investors should avoid is one that outlines the details of a company's participation in a corporate conference. In general, this news draws little attention to the stock, even when the conference is regarded as prestigious, and even when a special invitation is extended to the company's executives for participation.

An example of such news is given in this excerpt "... *(Company X) today announced that... President and Chief Executive Officer, has been selected to present in the "Update from Industry" session at the Heart Failure Congress 2011, organized by the Heart Failure Association of the European Society of Cardiology being held in Sweden..." (Source: BusinessWire).*

This press release clearly fits the "No Big Deals"—type of news. This is because the participation in the conference does not outline any details about the impact of this event on the company's market growth and business expansion, which are normally the main drivers of an unusual share price increase in reaction to a press release.

In general, the reaction of the market to this type of news is modest and cannot be sustained for a long period of time, even during the same intraday session following the press release. For the example quoted in this section, the market reaction resulted in a 12% increase in the share price in the immediate intraday session depicted in Figure 6.2.

Similar performances are typically exhibited for any other news that details a company's participation in a corporate conference. Therefore, unless small investors are interested in single digit percent gains on short-term investments, such news should be avoided, especially when the extended charts and quotes show no signs of undervaluation.

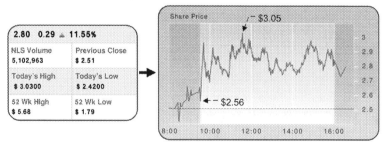

Figure 6.2. Intraday price chart showing the reaction of the market to news detailing the participation of a company in a corporate conference (*Source:* www.nasdaq.com)

6-3. EXHIBITIONS

Corporate exhibitions typically represent an opportunity for companies to showcase their new developments and draw market attention to their prospective products. However, from a trading perspective, the news that outlines participation in exhibitions rarely delineates the impact of such activity on the long-term market growth of the company.

In fact, the participation in a corporate exhibition does not necessarily mean that the company will be able to grow its business or tap into new markets as a consequence of this corporate activity. This uncertainty makes such press releases fit into the "No Big Deals"—type of news, which transpires into a modest positive momentum in the stock price in the immediate reaction to the news.

An example of such news is given in the following excerpt: ". . . *(Company X) announced today that the . . . Microwave Ablation System was featured at the Company's exhibition booth during the 6th Fire, Ice and Beyond: The Future of Ablation Therapies Educational Symposia. This Interventional Oncology Educational Symposia, accredited by the Accreditation Council for Continuing Medical Education, provided an advanced understanding of new and cutting-edge energy sources for tumor ablation . . ."* (*Source: BusinessWire*).

The significance of this press release does not extrapolate beyond the exhibition of the company's product at a booth during the referenced conference. However, whether or not this participation will physically impact the profits of the company and its business outlook remains uncertain, especially when no explicit connotations in this news hint to such prospects. It is this uncertainty that makes investors less attracted to this type of press releases, making their impact on the short-term momentum of the stock less substantial.

For the quoted example, the market reaction to the press release is equally modest as depicted in Figure 6.3. In this figure, the stock price gained 9% in the first minute of the intraday session, before losing momentum and closing the session up by only 1% from the opening price ($2.87).

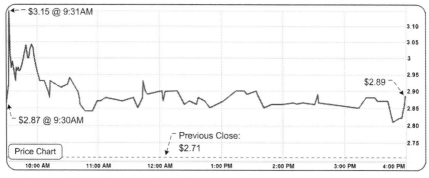

Figure 6.3. Intraday price chart showing the market reaction to a news release depicting the participation in a corporate exhibition (*Source:* finance.yahoo.com)

6-4.   PUBLICATIONS

Publications, whether business or scientific, also fit the "No Big Deals"—type of news. For scientific publications however, if the press release outlines new findings that may have a prospective market application, such news may become more significant if these applications are delineated explicitly in the press release. Otherwise, the market connotations will be speculative, and investors' reaction will be lessened by the uncertainty carried in the news.

To illustrate this contrast in an example, consider the following excerpt from a press release which reads as follows: ". . . *In a newly published paper, medical researchers at (Company X) report a diagnostic breakthrough in multiple sclerosis (MS), based on observations made possible by the company's unique . . . MRI (system).*

The findings reveal that the cause of multiple sclerosis may be biomechanical and related to earlier trauma to the neck, which can result in obstruction of the flow of cerebrospinal fluid (CSF) . . . The paper . . . has just been published and appears in the latest issue of the Journal of Physiological Chemistry and Physics and Medical NMR . . ." (*Source: PR Newswire*).

Despite the breakthrough that the company claims in this press release, a feel of uncertainty is evidenced in the content of the news. This is due to the report suggesting that the cause of multiple sclerosis *may be* biomechanical, and that those findings were based on observations and not on clinical data with statistical validation.

Even if these findings were published in a scientific article, the level of speculations with respect to the marketable aspect of these findings and the ability of the company to use them to grow its business is considerable. This speculative component typically lessens the interest in the stock on short-term basis.

In contrast, if the reported findings were based on a multi-phase clinical study with statistically validated data instead of pure observations, such news will be more compelling, even if the company did not explicitly outline a direct relationship between the significance of the data and its potential impact on the company's business and market growth.

However, because the publication is based on observations, the quoted press release fits into the "No Big Deals"—type of news and would not typically draw an unusual interest on the stock in the immediate reaction to the news. This is evidenced in Figure 6.4 which shows the price and volume charts of the stock in the session following the press release.

Figure 6.4. Intraday price and volume chart showing the market reaction to corporate news reporting the publication of new scientific findings
(*Source:* finance.yahoo.com)

With an opening price of $1.80 and a closing price of $1.81, a day-trader would have had little opportunities to generate any significant short-term profit from the market reaction to this news, especially on a low trading volume which increases the stock volatility as evidenced in the morning and afternoon price dips.

6-5.   INITIATION OF MEDICAL STUDIES

Other "No Big Deals"—type of news refers to the announcements made by public companies about the initiation of an activity that cannot be directly associated with any market growth. One of the examples that highlight the content of such news is the initiation of a medical study.

A sample of this news is given in the following excerpt: *"... (Company X) announced today the initiation of a Phase I clinical trial of the Company's lead drug candidate . . . in patients with refractory solid tumors. The trial is being conducted in collaboration with . . . a Research Institute in Nashville, Tennessee, following the approval of an Investigational New Drug (IND) application by the U.S. Food and Drug Administration (FDA) last month . . ." (Source: PR Newswire).*

The content of this news release contains no significant information beyond the announcement of the initiation of a clinical trial in collaboration with a research institute. However, this information alone is not enough to draw an unusual volume on the stock.

If instead, the news was reporting statistical clinical data about a medical breakthrough, or a successful completion of a clinical trial with positive results, the market reaction would have been more substantial, especially if the company's stocks show signs of undervaluation. But because this news is nothing more than an announcement, the reaction of the market was relatively insignificant as shown in Figure 6.5.

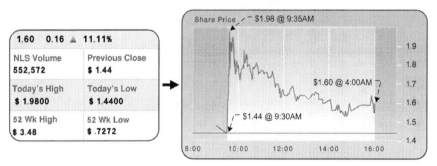

Figure 6.5. Intraday price chart showing the reaction of the market to news announcing the initiation of a medical study phase (*Source:* www.nasdaq.com)

Despite the early morning price ascent of 37% (from $1.44 to $1.98) during the first five minutes of the trading session, the upward intraday momentum of the stock was unsustainable by the news, where the stock closed the session up by only 11%. As a result, a day trader acquiring a stake in the early period of the intraday momentum would have most likely incurred a loss if the stake was sold at any subsequent time in the session.

A second example that highlights the recurrent aspect of the "No Big Deals"—type of news related to the initiation of a collaborative medical study is exhibited in the following excerpt: *". . . (Company X) announced today that it has entered into a three-party collaboration with the Yale School of Medicine and (Company Y) to explore the potential efficacy of investigational compounds identified by (Company X) and (Company Y) in their existing collaboration . . ."* (*Source: Global Newswire*).

The similarities between the two news releases are obvious, where the two reports announced the initiation of a collaborative medical study with a third-party institute. In the case of the second example, the collaboration is established with a university, which normally draws less attention from investors as compared to a collaboration with an industrial partner.

Nevertheless, the intraday price patterns in both cases shows similar trends, where in the case of the second example, the stock price jumped by 7% in the first fifteen minutes of the session before closing the day at only 3% (on an average volume).

6-6.   APPOINTMENTS

The last example discussed in this chapter refers to corporate news that outlines the details of a board member appointment or resignation. The reaction of the market to such news is not surprisingly transitory, as the press connotations fit exactly into the "No Big Deals" category. However, because of the recurrent aspect of these press releases, it becomes important to highlight them through an illustrative example, despite the relatively obvious aspect of their content.

An excerpt from a selected pertinent example reads as follows:

". . . (Company X) announced that . . . the Company's Executive Vice President and Chief Operating Officer, has retired from the Company . . . The Company also announced that . . . the Company's current Senior Vice President . . . has been named Executive Vice President and Chief Operating Officer . . ." (*Source: EDGAR Online*).

Clearly, this example fits into the "No Big Deals"—type of news where the announcement depicts an executive's resignation and a subsequent new appointment. The market reaction to this news is generally poor, except in some rare circumstances of major appointments for undervalued stocks, such as in the event where a majority shareholder is appointed as a board or executive member.

In such case, the market reaction to the news and the undervalued position of the stock may be more noticeable on short-term basis. In any other circumstances however, this news typically generates insignificant positive momentums on the stock, and thus should be avoided by short-term small investors.

6-7. OUTTAKE

In this chapter, a discussion on corporate news that generates no significant positive momentums on the stock market was presented. These press releases were labeled as the "No Big Deals"—type of news which exhibit a modest impact on the short-term performance of the stock.

The examples discussed in this chapter highlighted the significance of this recommendation. For short-term investors, these examples should serve as a basis for the analysis of any other corporate news that fits into this identified category.

Small investors should avoid trading positions with stocks marked by such press releases, as their content cannot sustain a significant positive price momentum on short-term basis. This recommendation also extends to positive stock momentums which are not explicitly supported by any press release that justifies the upward trend.

Chapter 7

RECURRENT INTRADAY PRICE CHART TRENDS

7-1.   INTRODUCTION

Price charts serve as an important indicator of the stock's momentum and its tendency to gain or lose value on an intraday basis. In many cases, an experienced investor can anticipate the performance of the stock or its reaction to a news release through a visual analysis of its daily price chart.

Many of the price chart trends tend to be recurrent. Most notably, trends associated with the movement of a stock in reaction to a press release become very significant in enabling short-term investors to schedule the execution of their buying or selling positions.

While buying positions can be originated with great confidence based on corporate news interpretation, selling positions are much harder to formulate on intraday basis. This is due to the lack of reliable analysis tools that enable a deterministic detection of the peak intraday price threshold. In fact, most selling strategies are probabilistic, and their accuracy depends on other speculative or unquantifiable psychological factors such as investors' desire to assume risk in the hope of a better selling opportunity.

For day-traders however, understanding the dynamics of price charts can serve as a solid foundation for strengthening the soundness of a buying position, anticipating the daily saturation level of the intraday stock price, and formulating short-term holding or selling positions.

In this chapter, a discussion on the most recurrent and reliable intraday price chart trends is presented to support investors' buying, selling, and holding positions formulated based on news interpretation. The discussion is generic, in the sense that the illustrated trends are not necessarily tied to any specific corporate news. Instead, they are broadly applicable to the analysis of intraday price chart dynamics generated in reaction to any press release that sustains an upward momentum on the stock price.

7-2.   STAIR-LIKE ASCENT

A stair-like ascending behavior of a stock price is based on the fundamental market dynamics of *support* and *resistance*, and represents a signal for a safe sustained upward price momentum.

In a stair-like behavior, the stock price tends to stabilize at a threshold for a certain period of time before pulling either up or down, depending upon the nature of the flat threshold. In the event of a resistance threshold, the share price will tend to pull back until a new support level is reached from which an attempt to regain price value can be initiated.

In the event of a support threshold, the price will be sustained, and a continual upward momentum on the stock will be observed until a new resistance level is reached. An example of such stair-like formation is depicted in Figure 7.1 which shows a factual price chart (*left*) and its equivalent simplified straight-line approximation (*right*).

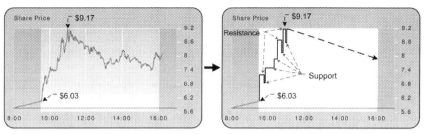

Figure 7.1. Price chart (*left*) with its equivalent simplified straight-line approximation (*right*) highlighting the stair-like ascent and the support and resistance levels (*Source for the left chart:* www.nasdaq.com)

This type of stair-like behavior is typical of any ascending price chart on the market. In some cases, the stair-like shape is easily recognized such as in the example of Figure 7.1. In other cases, the flat threshold intervals are either brief, or largely extended that the recognition of the stair-like behavior may not be as obvious as in the example of Figure 7.1. In both cases however, investors formulating their trading strategies on news interpretation should also schedule the execution of their buying orders at a support interval in case the early morning opportunity at the opening of the intraday session was missed.

Although detecting the onset of a support phase is arduous in general and requires experience and training, some support intervals are easier to detect visually than others. These are normally the ones initiated after a slump in the stock price (for example, the first support interval following the first resistance threshold in the approximated straight-line chart of Figure 7.1).

7-3. EARLY MORNING SLUMP

Another trend that reflects the potential strength of a stock in response to a positive press release is the morning price slump. This slump is typically an indication of strength, as opposed to the momentum of a significant pre-market ascent which is normally unsustainable in the intraday session.

The dynamics of a price slump is depicted in Figure 7.2, which shows a stock dipping in the early minutes of the intraday session prior to the initiation of an ascending momentum. When this dip occurs, it typically follows a pre-market ascent, and it normally reflects the tendency of day-traders to lower the opening price of the stock in anticipation of a major subsequent spike.

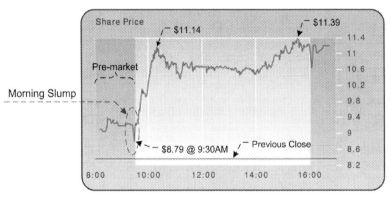

Figure 7.2. Price chart showing the morning slump that precedes a price ascent on positive news (*Source:* www.nasdaq.com)

Such dip happens quickly, and allows the stock to reset some of the gains established in the pre-market session. This in turn enables day-traders, who cannot participate in the pre-market activities, to maximize their intraday profit by taking advantage of a buying opportunity established near the closing price of the previous session as a result of the morning slump.

This slump however is not always a sign of strength. In fact, when the stock's upward momentum is not sustained by a positive press release, the early morning slump may rather be a sign of weakness. Short-term investors are therefore encouraged to analyze the news generating the stock momentum before formulating a buying position at the end of the morning slump, whenever such slump occurs.

7-4. SHORT-TERM SELLING TACTICS BASED ON SATURATION ZONES

Scheduling the execution of a selling position in a stock is an important factor for profit maximization. Normally, the ideal instance for placing a selling order is at the peak threshold of the intraday price chart. Nonetheless, detecting the onset of this peak price threshold is significantly difficult.

In general, it is a relatively deterministic task for educated investors to anticipate the positive reaction of a stock to a specific press release, and to time the placement of a buying order accordingly. In contrast, predicting the extent by which the press release will impact the upward momentum of the stock is a more difficult and probabilistic task that is also subject to speculations.

This speculative nature of the intraday peak price threshold increases the risk exposure for investors as they wait for the onset of the next better selling opportunity. In many cases, a higher peak never occurs, and investors lose significantly on their initially-profitable buying positions as a consequence of these speculations.

To avoid this risk exposure, many investors choose to cap their gains at a pre-determined threshold. For instance, an investor might decide to sell a buying position when the value of the stock increases by 10%. While this conservative approach can minimize the risk of losses if the shares were otherwise held for a longer period of time, it may equally demolish the opportunity for any additional potential gains that may occur subsequently during the session if the stock continues its upward momentum.

One of the relatively reliable approaches to avoid premature selling, and to maximize intraday profit is to schedule the execution of a selling position at a price saturation zone. This zone can be detected visually on the intraday price chart, and consists of two consecutive peak resistance levels separated by a support level initiated after a considerable slump in the price.

An example of a price saturation zone is shown in Figure 7.3. The duration of this zone is normally short, and can be detected graphically by monitoring the onset of a systematic series of consecutive resistance and support levels.

Typically, when the price chart follows an ascending trajectory, it often reaches a peak level (1st peak in Figure 7.3) where the resistance is so high that the price slumps considerably shortly thereafter. This noticeable slump relative to others is a first signal of saturation.

However, the stock price normally finds another support level from which a new recovery ascent is initiated. If this ascent manages to break through the established first saturation level, then the stock may still carry extra momentum to gain further value. In contrast, if the stock price shows signs of weakness during the recovery ascent and tends to backtrack from the upward momentum, a new peak will be formed (2nd peak in Figure 7.3) which will signal the end of the saturation zone.

At the end of this zone, the tendency of the stock to lose value will outweigh that of gaining value, and the price would normally never return to this saturation level again. This means that, unless a buying position is sold at the end of the saturation zone (at the 2nd peak), an investor will likely never get another selling opportunity at a price close to the ultimate peak established during the intraday session.

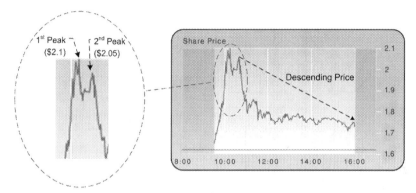

Figure 7.3. Intraday price chart showing the onset of a saturation zone, with a close-up view of its consecutive peaks and the subsequent price slump at the end of the zone (*Source:* www.nasdaq.com)

In line with these price chart dynamics, short-term traders are recommended to sell their position at the end of the saturation zone. This conservative tactic, not only offers investors the ability to sell their stocks at a price that is close to the ultimate peak of the day (which is normally difficult to detect), but also shields them from the risk of significant losses which normally follow the end of the saturation zone as evidenced in the example of Figure 7.3.

The significance of this recommendation is depicted in a second example shown in Figure 7.4 which highlights the recurrent nature of the saturation zone. The similarities between the two examples are obvious, where in both cases, the stock establishes an ultimate peak price (1st price), then backtracks noticeably before initiating a second peak that signals the end of the saturation zone.

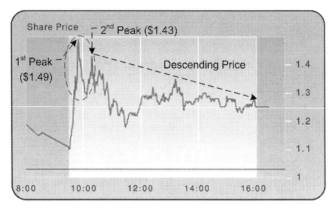

Figure 7.4. Intraday price chart highlighting the recurrent aspect of price saturation zones (*Source:* www.nasdaq.com)

This recurrent aspect of saturation zones makes them a reliable choice for conservative selling tactics. By adopting this technique, investors maximize their profit by selling their position at the onset of the 2nd peak, which enables them to avoid the risks associated with the descending phase of the stock that typically follows a saturation zone.

7-5.   SHORT-TERM SELLING TACTICS BASED ON STRIDE LENGTH

Another selling tactic aimed at maximizing short-term profit attempts to detect the onset of the peak price threshold of the intraday session by monitoring the length of individual price strides during an upward momentum.

A price stride, by definition, is the price gain that a stock achieves between one support level and the following resistance or support level. An example of these price strides is shown in Figure 7.5 which depicts the price chart of the same example shown earlier in Figure 7.3.

As the stock follows an upward trend, the length of a price stride tends to vary proportionally to the momentum that the stock carries during the ascent. If the momentum is high, the price strides tend to be long. However, as the momentum starts to slow down, the price strides tend to become shorter when the resistance on the upward movement becomes more significant.

These dynamics are illustrated in Figure 7.5, which shows a stock ascent consisting of four different stride phases. The first two strides are long as the stock gains quick value from $1.62 to $2.02 (+25%). However, after the second stride, the momentum starts to lessen resulting in a shorter third and fourth stride. This last fourth stride is obviously the shortest, and is followed by a considerable dip in the price after establishing the peak of the intraday session.

Such behavior normally characterizes the stride lengths of a price chart, where the likelihood of a price retreat increases with the shorter strides, making the tactic of monitoring the length of consecutive strides a valuable visual tool for investors to anticipate the onset of the peak price of the day.

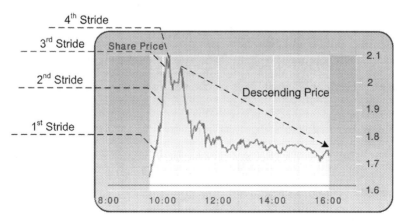

Figure 7.5. Intraday price chart showing the difference in stride lengths as the positive trend gradually loses upward momentum (*Source:* www.nasdaq.com)

This peak price typically occurs in the region that encompasses the shortest stride. Therefore, by adopting the tactic of stride lengths, investors maximize their day profit by selling their position in the region of the shortest stride which directly precedes the price dip that constitutes the saturation zone.

7-6.   ASCENDING STOCKS ON POSITIVE NEWS

The decision of holding a short-term position in a stock for more than one consecutive trading session depends on multiple market factors. In Chapter 4, the recommendation of holding a stock for an extended period of time was based on the interpretation of corporate news for strong positive market connotations that can sustain a continual upward momentum on the stock.

In addition to this interpretation, the intraday shape of the price chart during a session marked by a major press release can also be indicative of the stock performance in the subsequent sessions. For example, a price chart that peaks at the end of the intraday hours will likely maintain some aspects of this ascent during the next-day session.

The rationale behind this behavior is based on the price saturation dynamics explained earlier in section 7-4. In fact, when the intraday share price peaks at the end of the session such as in the example shown in Figure 7.6(A), a saturation threshold would have not been established for that session.

This means that the price ascent driven by strong corporate news would *likely* extend to the subsequent session until a saturation level is established as shown in Figure 7.6(B) (at $7.50). In such case, holding the stock for the next session would potentially generate additional profit (a strong after-hour performance and an undervalued position of the stock further strengthen the likelihood of this next-day profit).

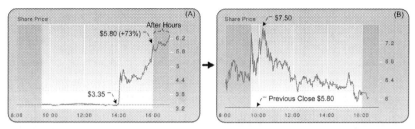

Figure 7.6. An illustration of an ascending stock price with a peak established at the end of the trading session (A), and the continual early morning ascent in the following session (B) (*Source:* www.nasdaq.com)

However, investors must be careful about the volatile aspect of the stock during that session, as the continual price ascent can normally *only* be sustained during the early intraday minutes before losing momentum and dipping to lower thresholds. The example in Figure 7.6 (A & B) serves as a good factual illustration of this behavior.

7-7. DESCENDING STOCKS ON POSITIVE NEWS

Price charts can also be indicative of the stock's tendency to lose value in the subsequent sessions following a press release. In many cases for instance, positive news with strong market connotations can only sustain a short significant ascent in the stock price, which typically occurs in the first hour of the intraday session. After this early ascent, the stock price continually loses value to close the session at a price considerably lower than the established intraday peak.

The example shown earlier in Figure 7.5, and the current example shown in Figure 7.7 serve as a good illustration of this dynamic. In the event of such descending trend on positive news, investors are recommended not to hold the stock past the end of the intraday session despite the positivity reflected in the news.

This is because stocks marked by this behavior will most likely lose value in the following sessions as illustrated in Figure 7.7, where a descending stock (on positive news) is shown to continue its descent during the subsequent trading session.

In fact, if a positive press release is unable to sustain a prolonged price ascent in the trading session that immediately follows the press release, it will be unlikely that such news (alone) will be capable of generating an upward momentum on the stock during the subsequent sessions. This means that non-speculative investors buying stakes in the stock as a result of the positive corporate news will have no interest in holding their position—based on hopes that the next trading session will bring better news—because the descending trend will likely extend to the following sessions.

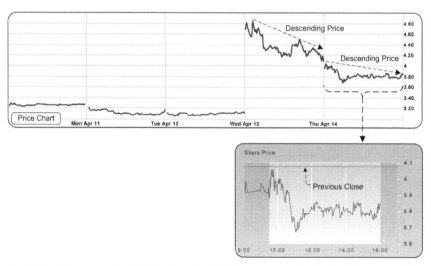

Figure 7.7. A composite illustration showing the descent of a stock price on positive news that cannot sustain an upward price momentum in the immediate session following the press release (*Sources:* finance.yahoo.com & www.nasdaq.com)

7-8.   OUTAKE

In this chapter, a discussion of the most reliable techniques for scheduling the execution of short-term selling positions was presented.

Unlike buying positions which can be originated with great confidence based on news interpretation and extended price chart analysis, selling positions are more difficult to formulate on intraday basis. This is because the anticipation of the peak daily price threshold is a probabilistic event which carries a speculative component that depends on the investors' desire to assume risk in the hope of a better selling opportunity.

The tactics presented in this chapter help to mitigate such risk exposure, and provide a safe outlet for short-term investors to maximize their intraday profit, while shielding their positions from significant losses that may be incurred by holding a position unnecessarily long.

These techniques apply to any stock, irrespective of the nature of the press release. Thus, it is recommended that short-term investors employ such tools to minimize risk exposure and maximize short-term profit by analyzing intraday price charts for daily signs of strength and/or saturation.

PART B

MARKET RESEARCH

Chapter 8

OVERVIEW OF TECHNICAL CHART ANALYSIS

In the first part of this book, the discussion focused on the non-technical aspect of stock trading by introducing short-term online investors to trading strategies that are based on corporate news and visual chart interpretation. The objective of this part was to appeal to the broader readership of individual stock investors, by simplifying the approach of market analysis to a sensible news-based interpretation without the prerequisite of technical and statistical chart examination.

In the second part of this book, the focus is on the technical aspect of the stock market. The discussion in this part serves as a brief introduction to the motivations of technical analysis, and to the different technical charting styles and market indicators employed by traders to anticipate the behavior of the market. The main objective of this part is to introduce market researchers to a new experimental software platform called SMART. This platform enables free access to discrete-time intraday stock data that represents the foundations of all technical and statistical market analysis tools.

8-1.   DEFINITION OF TECHNICAL ANALYSIS

Technical analysis is the practice of forecasting the future movement of a stock based on past and current price and volume information. The underlying foundation of this analysis is a combination of mathematical and statistical models that extrapolate existing information into a likelihood of a prospective event, the latter being a price ascent, decline or saturation.

The science of technical analysis is often compared to weather forecasting where the forecasted event is subject to prediction errors. Particularly, in technical analysis applications, the reliability of market models is highly inconsistent as the behavior of the market does not follow any scientifically validated phenomena. This predictive effort is made even more arduous by the susceptibility of the stock market to many unpredictable events that range from unquantifiable investors' emotions to natural disasters such as earthquakes.

In general, the science of technical analysis relies on three major principles. The first principle assumes that the causal price and volume fluctuations of a security can be modeled with mathematical equations. These equations and formulas generate a statistically reliable indication of the stock performance over a pre-defined time frame which could range from a few minutes, all the way back to the original public offering (IPO) of the security.

The second principle states that technical analysis is based on the market's deterministic information (price and volume), and not on the factors that initiate a specific reaction on the market. This means that technical analysis does not take into consideration any collateral factors such as press releases or geo-political events.

The third principle of technical analysis is based on the common understanding that market trends are recurrent, and that history repeats itself, where the chart patterns generated in response to a specific set of circumstances will duplicate themselves whenever similar circumstances are furnished again.

At the core of technical analysis is historical market data that defines the established record of a given security (stock). This data is modeled mathematically and overlaid on a time-chart as a price or volume indicator that depicts prospective information about the security's trending potential, and the probability of its direction and continuation.

8-2. FORMS OF TECHNICAL ANALYSIS

The price of a security is the key driver of technical analysis. In market theories, many definitions exist for a security price. The most logical of these is that the *price* defines the sum value of all positions (bullish, bearish, neutral) held by market participants, which in turn delineates the market agreement on the fairest price to buy or sell the security.

As new developments occur on the market, the price tends to adjust itself, by either increasing or decreasing in value depending upon the nature of the stimulus. In general, the role that the price value and its daily fluctuations play in technical analysis can be divided into three different views.

8-2-1. Strong View: Technicians

In the strong form of technical analysis, the price value is seen as carrying all available information about the security. This includes publicly explicit information, as well as inside information privy to executives and management boards. Technicians therefore believe that all traders are privileged to the same corporate information which is carried by the price value of the security.

8-2-2. Semi-Strong View: Random Walkers

In the semi-strong form of market analysis, the price of a security reflects all readily available explicit information. This includes corporate news and other activities such as SEC filings and earnings reports. However, the semi-strong view also implies that implicit information not made available to the public is not reflected in the security's price.

This information is used by insider traders to derive profit at the discretion of public traders. The random walk theory therefore implies that the only outlet to generating profit on the market is through insider trading. The rationale is based on the notion that, by the time the inside information becomes public, the security price would have already adjusted itself to reflect the impact of this information, thus leaving no measurable opportunities for public traders to benefit from these new developments.

8-2-3.   Weak View: Fundamentalists

The fundamentalists' view of market analysis states that the current price of a security is only a reflection of a combination of past prices and corporate developments, and that the prospective price cannot be forecasted by analyzing prior information alone.

The only use of prior price record is to ascertain the current position of the security, and to detect any abnormalities in the current price which may reflect either an undervalued, or an overvalued position of the security. Buying and selling strategies are therefore based on the interpretation of these abnormalities through financial models.

Because all three aforementioned forms exhibit fundamental differences in their views, a more conservative form of the role of price values in determining the prospective price of a security is one that combines views from both the semi-strong and the weak forms.

This view implies that the current price of a security is a reflection of existing public information, and that it is virtually impossible to predict the future price based on analyzing prior price records alone.

Only new information will impact the price of a security, which seems to be a sensible view judging by the reaction of the market to corporate news as outlined in Part *A* of this book.

8-3. CHARTING STYLES

In analyzing the current position of a security and its prospective price outlook, analysts adopt multiple chart visualization techniques which help illustrate price variations over a chosen period of time. For intraday charts, the data reflects the price variations from the opening to the closing of the trading session. For extended charts, the data visualizes the closing price of a chosen sequence of consecutive trading sessions, or a combination of price data such as opening, highs, lows and closing prices (for example).

The most common of these charting styles is the line chart which was employed exclusively in the examples presented in Part *A*. However, many other chart visualization techniques exist, which highlight essential components of price patterns such as trend lines and support or resistance levels. Some of these most distinctive techniques will be discussed in the following sections.

8-3-1. Candlesticks

Candlestick charts originated from the rice traders of Japan in the seventeenth century, and visualize a progression of opening and closing prices for a chosen time period, along with the high and low bounds of the price during every trading session in the sequence.

The basic components of a candlestick chart are the body and the shadows (Figure 8.1). The body is a rectangular illustration whose horizontal edges depict the opening and closing prices of a security during a given trading session. If the closing price is higher than the opening price, the body will be filled with a solid hatch (green color normally, depending upon the source), with the upper horizontal edge denoting the closing price, and the lower horizontal edge denoting the opening price.

However, if the closing price is lower than the opening price, the body will be either hollow, or filled with a solid hatch (red color for example, depending upon the source) and the interpretation of the horizontal edges will be flipped. This means that, in this case, the upper edge will denote the opening price, while the lower edge will denote the closing price of the security on a given trading session. The length of the body also serves as an illustration of the amount of price gain or loss during every trading session; the higher the gain (or the loss), the longer the height of the body.

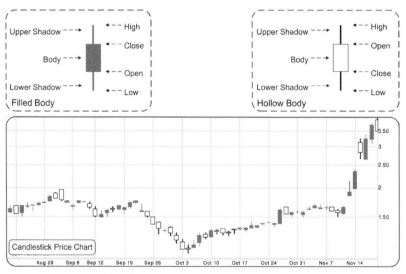

Figure 8.1. Candlestick price chart with close-ups showing the nomenclature of a filled and a hollow body (*Source:* finance.yahoo.com)

The shadows on the other hand are a reflection of the highest and lowest price achieved during a given trading session. The upper shadow denotes the highest price, while the lower shadow denotes the lowest price reached during the session.

The length of the bodies and the shadows can therefore serve as a visual indication of the buying (support) and selling (resistance) pressure, as well as the price bounds of every trading session in a selected sequence, respectively.

8-3-2.   Kagi Charts

Kagi charts also originated from Japan and are made of thin and thick vertical lines connected together by short horizontal lines with the objective of reducing random price noise. As the price of a security fluctuates over a period of time, a Kagi chart adds a new vertical line only when the price has reversed enough to cancel the current upward or downward trend.

Until such reversal happens, the price patterns in a Kagi chart will move either up or down in their current column. As such, Kagi charts do not have equally spaced columns since the width of a column depends on the onset of trend reversal actions. An example of a Kagi chart with a combination of thin and thick lines is shown in Figure 8.2.

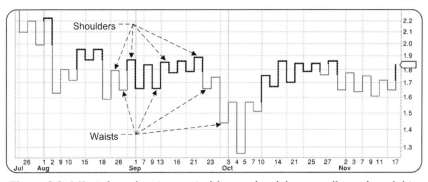

Figure 8.2. A Kagi chart showing vertical (upward and downward) trends and thin and thick lines (*Source:* www.stockcharts.com)

In a Kagi chart, the thick lines are called *yang*, and the thin lines are called *yin*. The thickness of the lines changes anytime a vertical line reaches and surpasses the high of the previous horizontal line on an upward trend, or the low of the previous horizontal line on a downward trend.

These lines will continue to move vertically up or down until prices reverse by a pre-defined amount, typically by 4%. When that happens, a horizontal line is added to connect two trends of different directions.

The location where this transition happens is either called a *shoulder* if the shift happens from an upward vertical trend to a downward vertical trend, or a *waist* if the transition happens from a downward to an upward trend.

From a trading perspective, Kagi charts are employed to visualize buying and selling opportunities. One of the most common approaches to formulate such positions is to schedule a buying order at the onset of the *yang* line, and a selling order at the onset of the *yin* line.

8-3-3.   Renko Charts

The term Renko originated from the word *Ranga*, which signifies *brick* in Japanese. As such, a Renko chart illustrates a diagonal sequential cascade of hollow and filled bricks plotted against a selected time period, where the spacing along the time-axis is not uniform.

A brick in a Renko chart has a pre-determined size, known as a point-scale, which defines the height of the brick. Anytime the price swings fill the entire height of the prospective brick, a new one is added to the chart. This brick will be visualized with a hollow rectangle if the price trend is positive, or with a solid hatch if the trend is negative.

To illustrate the dynamics of a Renko chart with an example, consider a four-point scale with a given security whose price is changing from $48 to $51. If the top horizontal edge of the last brick in the sequence is at $46, a new hollow brick will be added to the Renko chart since the top edge of this new brick will correspond to $50 (46+4), which is entirely bounded by the price fluctuation range of $48 to $51.

However, a second hollow brick with a lower horizontal edge at $50 and an upper edge at $54 will not be added to the chart because the price of $54 is not included in the $48-$51 range.

With this technique, the lower horizontal edge of the current brick will coincide with the upper horizontal edge of the preceding brick in an upward Renko trend. Similarly, the upper edge of the current brick will coincide with the lower edge of the preceding brick in a downward Renko trend. This generates a diagonal visualization of price upward and downward patterns as shown in the sample illustration of Figure 8.3.

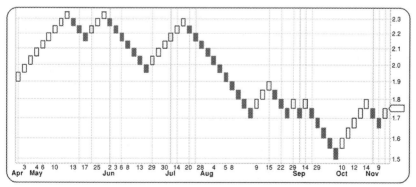

Figure 8.3. Sample Renko chart showing hollow and filled bricks which depict upward and downward price trends, respectively (*Source:* www.stockcharts.com)

139

Because of the nature of a Renko chart, prices may not change for a significant period of time. The length of this steady period depends directly on the selected point scale. Furthermore, the current price depicted on a Renko chart is often less than the actual security price. This is because prices will be trimmed to the nearest top (in an upward trend) or bottom (in a downward trend) horizontal edge of the latest brick until the entire height of the next brick is filled by the price fluctuation range.

With these visualization techniques, Renko charts are most useful in visualizing bullish (hollow bricks) and bearish (filled bricks) trends. Buying and selling activities are scheduled based on these trends, where technical investors often postpone their respective trading actions until two or three identical bricks are formed in the sequence.

8-4. CHART PATTERNS

Chart patterns enable investors to make short-term and long-term forecasts based on intraday or extended price data. Because of the significant buying and selling activities on the market, chart patterns are employed as visual tools to expose upward and downward price trends, and put in perspective the forces of supply and demand that drive the market's momentum.

Many chart patterns have been investigated and developed over the years to simplify the analysis of price charts. In this section, the discussion will focus on four main patterns which are widely employed in markets' technical analyses.

8-4-1. Head and Shoulder Top/Bottom Reversal

A head and shoulder top reversal trend forms during a price uptrend. Its completion marks the end of a positive momentum and typically signals a trend reversal. The dynamics of this pattern are characterized by three successive peaks. The middle peak is the highest of the three (the head), with the remaining two peaks saturating at an almost equal price (the shoulders).

To recognize a head and shoulder top reversal pattern on a price chart, one should first establish a price uptrend. While in this uptrend, the first left shoulder creates a first peak which is followed by a price decline that does not break through the price trend line.

The price would then advance from the low of this decline to establish a new peak that saturates at a higher price than the top of the left shoulder. A similar price descent ensues, which typically stabilizes around a bottom price that is almost even with the first bottom. A line connecting the two bottoms establishes the neckline of the head and shoulder pattern as illustrated in Figure 8.4(A).

When the second descent stabilizes, the price tries to regain value only to saturate at a new peak which establishes the right shoulder. The peak of this second shoulder is typically in line with the high of the left shoulder. Beyond this peak, the trend usually reverses, and the price breaks through the established neckline signaling a bearish momentum that prompts investors to sell their positions.

A head and shoulder bottom reversal trend on the other hand represents the opposite of the top reversal trend and occurs during a price downtrend. Its completion typically marks the beginning of a positive momentum.

A bottom reversal trend contains three troughs with the middle one being the deepest. The dynamics of this pattern start with a first depression in a price downtrend that marks the left shoulder. After the establishment of this shoulder, the price typically regains value before saturating and dropping again to establish a new depression.

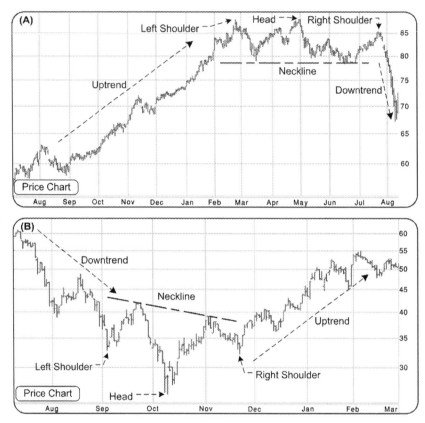

Figure 8.4. Head and Shoulder patterns, (A) Top Reversal, (B) Bottom Reversal
(*Source:* finance.yahoo.com)

This second depression is deeper than the first one and creates the head of the pattern. From this head, the price regains momentum before saturating at a price level in line with the peak of the first shoulder. After this saturation, the price drops again to establish the second shoulder of the pattern (Figure 8.4(B)).

The neckline of this pattern connects the peaks of the first and second shoulders. In a typical head and shoulder bottom reversal pattern, the price breaks through the neckline after the second shoulder (Figure 8.4(B)). This signals a bullish upward momentum and a buying opportunity for investors.

8-4-2.   Double Top/Bottom Reversal

A double top reversal pattern consists of two equal peaks separated by a modest trough in the middle. Typically, this pattern is noticeable on extended price charts where the duration of the middle trough should be no less than one month.

This pattern follows an uptrend where the first peak is established when the positive momentum faces resistance and drops moderately (10% to 20%) to new support levels. Subsequent to this depression, a new peak is established at a relatively lower volume until the price meets resistance from the previous peak.

This makes the second peak saturate at a level that is in line with the earlier peak. When this happens, the pattern reverses, and the price breaks through the support line of the middle trough to initiate a downtrend, prompting investors to relinquish their holding positions. A sample illustration reflecting the dynamics of a double top reversal pattern is shown in Figure 8.5(A).

In a similar fashion, a double bottom reversal pattern can be recognized on extended charts that reflect a price downtrend. This pattern consists of two consecutive troughs of near equal depth, separated by a moderate peak in the middle.

When the first depression of the bottom reversal pattern occurs, it typically marks the end of the downtrend, and it is followed by brief gains as the price finds new support at the bottom of the trough.

However, this gain soon faces resistance and turns into a second depression that creates a second trough.

Figure 8.5. Double Top/Bottom Reversal patterns, (A) Top Reversal, (B) Bottom Reversal (*Source:* finance.yahoo.com)

The bottom of this trough typically levels with the earlier bottom established at the end of the first trough. Subsequent to this second trough, the stock price gains momentum and breaks through the resistance line established at the peak of the moderate middle recovery trend. Once this happens, the price trend finds enough support to maintain an uptrend that signals a buying opportunity for investors. These dynamics of the double bottom reversal pattern and the subsequent uptrend are reflected in the example of Figure 8.5(B).

8-4-3. Rising/Falling Wedge

The connotations of a rising wedge are similar to those of the stride length's selling tactics introduced in section 7-5 (Chapter 7). Indeed, a rising wedge is a price trend that begins wide at the bottom and contracts as prices move higher to meet increasing resistance.

A rising wedge is typically a selling pattern that forms over a period of three to six months. This period is required to allow the intermediate peaks that create these patterns to form and mature, making them noticeable as complete rising wedge patterns by chart analysts.

The dynamics of a rising wedge pattern are characterized by at least two consecutive peaks, where the saturation level of the last peak is higher than that of the previous peak in the sequence. Every time the price peaks, it typically relinquishes some of the gains to create a trough from which a new ascent is initiated. As the price continues its upward momentum, the vertical distance that separates a trough from the subsequent peak becomes shorter, and the price meets a higher resistance level that causes it to contract.

A resistance line will be formed by joining at least two peaks in the pattern with the top of the last peak being higher than that of the preceding one. A support line will also be formed by joining at least two support levels, where the last support reaction of this line occurs at a lower level than the preceding one as illustrated in Figure 8.6(A).

At the onset of the contraction zone, the price uptrend will not typically establish a new peak, and the resistance level of the contraction zone causes it to start declining. When this downtrend breaks through the established support line, a trend reversal ensues signaling a bearish momentum to investors.

Figure 8.6. Wedge Patterns, (A) Rising Wedge Reversal, (B) Falling Wedge Reversal
(*Source:* finance.yahoo.com)

In contrast to a rising wedge, a falling wedge pattern follows a downtrend that starts wide at the top and contracts as prices descend to lower levels. Two support and resistance lines delimit the pattern, where the support line joins the bottoms of at least two troughs, and the resistance line joins the highs of at least two peaks in the pattern. With the resistance line however, one of the highs should correspond to the peak of the wide section at the beginning of the pattern.

These two lines typically converge towards a zone of higher support as shown in Figure 8.6(B). Thus, as the price continues to move downwards towards the convergence zone, a contraction in the price fluctuations between the peaks and the bottoms occurs. This contracting behavior signals a trend reversal.

This trend reversal should be supported by a higher volume towards the end of the contraction zone. If this happens, the price will typically exhibit an uptrend that breaks through the established resistance line signaling a bullish momentum for investors.

8-4-4.   Ascending/Descending Triangles

Ascending triangles represent a recurrent sequence of cumulative reaction highs and lows that signal a continuation of the current uptrend. Among all patterns, triangles are easier to recognize visually on a price chart, and can be used as short-term or long term price indicators.

In an uptrend, an ascending triangular pattern exhibits two or more equal highs which form a near horizontal line at the top. The bottoms of the troughs in this pattern form an oblique line that points in the direction of the uptrend. This ascending line joins two or more trough lows and converges towards the top line as the price moves upwards. This price rise is accompanied by a decline in volume as the pattern matures.

Typically, the declining volume indicates the potentiality of an upside breakout signaling a buying opportunity for investors. This breakout represents a spike in the price that precedes a subsequent decline as shown in the example of Figure 8.7(A).

A descending triangle on the other hand represents the opposite of an ascending triangular pattern. That is, a descending triangle is a recurrent formation in a downtrend that signals continuation of the bearish momentum. In this pattern, two or more comparable trough lows create the lower horizontal trend line. Similarly, two or more comparable peaks form the top descending trend line which converges towards the horizontal line as shown in Figure 8.7(B).

Figure 8.7. Triangular patterns, (A) Ascending Triangles, (B) Descending Triangles (*Source:* finance.yahoo.com)

The convergence zone is marked by a decrease in volume that signals the maturity of the trend. When this happens, a downside break ensues, and the price starts falling considerably below the horizontal support line signaling a selling opportunity for investors.

8-5.   MARKET INDICATORS AND OVERLAYS

Technical indicators represent a sequence of data points generated using mathematical and statistical formulas applied to the price and volume data of a security. Indicators that share the same scale as that of the price chart are plotted directly on top of this chart, and are thus dubbed overlays.

Price data employed in the calculation of technical indicators consists of any combination of the open, close, high and low prices of a security over a selected period of consecutive trading sessions. Technical indicators can also be calculated based on intraday price and volume data.

In all cases however, the objective of market indicators is to attempt to forecast the prospective direction of a security by filtering and analyzing price data in order to expose buying and selling opportunities. These indicators deliver the most reliable prediction when the signals they generate are coupled with an analysis of price chart patterns.

In general, existing technical indicators are agglomerated into two major categories. The first category encompasses the *Leading Indicators*, which lead the market's price direction by employing prior data to estimate future directions. The second category encompasses the *Lagging Indicators*, which follow the market action and adjust to changes in the price after such variations have occurred.

A broad example of a leading indicator is the Federal Reserve's interest rates which directly impact the health of the economy and the direction of the market. A broad example of a lagging indicator on the other hand is the unemployment rate which is impacted subsequently by the health of the economy.

From a trading perspective, many technical indicators are employed as a short-term investment compass to expose opportunities, and enable traders to formulate buying and selling positions. Some of these most common indictors are the moving average convergence-divergence indicator (MACD), the relative strength index (RSI) and the Bollinger bands.

8-5-1. Moving Average Convergence-Divergence Indicator (MACD)

Moving averages represent the basis of the MACD indicator. By definition, moving averages are statistical filters that smooth out the noisiness of a price chart. They do not generate any market prediction, but rather identify the current direction with a lag as their calculation is based on past price data. The order of the moving average depicts the number of the trading periods used in the calculation of its value.

In the MACD indicator, one of the overlays is the 12-day exponential moving average also known as the *shorter average*. The other line represents the 26-day exponential moving average, which is also dubbed the *longer average*. The resulting MACD line is the difference between the shorter and the longer average as illustrated in Figure 8.8.

Convergence occurs when the two averages move closer towards each other. Divergence occurs otherwise. When the shorter average is leading the longer average, the MACD is positive, and its value increases as the gap between the two averages widens. This signals an uptrend momentum.

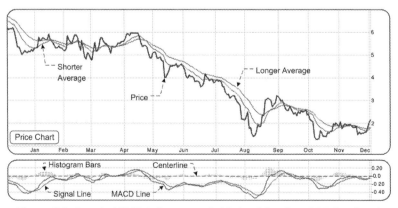

Figure 8.8. Sample MACD indicator with 12-day (short) and 26-day (long) exponential moving average price overlays (*Source:* finance.yahoo.com)

Negative MACD values indicate that the shorter average is trailing the longer average, which signals a down-trending price momentum. In general, the interpretation of the MACD indicator is based on two major observations. The first observation refers to the instance of the *signal line* cross-over, while the second observation refers to the instance of the *centerline* cross-over.

The signal line (Figure 8.8), by definition, represents the 9-day exponential moving average of the MACD line. A bullish momentum is therefore signaled when the MACD line crosses the signal line in the upward direction. A bearish momentum is signaled when the crossover occurs in the downward direction.

An oscillating histogram is created by subtracting the MACD line from the signal line. This histogram is composed of positive and negative bars that oscillate around a zero centerline. The magnitude of each bar depicts the difference between the MACD and the signal line at a given instance in time.

A bullish momentum is signaled anytime the MACD line moves above the centerline. This happens when the shorter average crosses and surpasses the longer average. In contrast, a bearish momentum is initiated anytime the MACD line drops below the zero centerline, which occurs when the shorter average trails the longer average and signals a selling opportunity for investors.

8-5-2. `Relative Strength Index (RSI)

The relative strength index is a momentum oscillator that measures the amplitude and speed of change of directional price variations. The calculation of the RSI is typically based on a 14-day timeframe. However, this timeframe can be increased or decreased to modify the index sensitivity to price fluctuations. The RSI can also be calculated for intraday data as shown in the example of Figure 8.9.

The RSI chart oscillates between 0 and 100. The index is considered overbought when the RSI value exceeds 70, and oversold when the RSI value drops below 20. These thresholds can be further adjusted to better fit a given security or the market-type for which the RSI is calculated.

The RSI chart can also indicate the imminence of a market turning point. This is technically known as divergence, where a bearish divergence occurs when the price establishes a new high but the RSI makes a lower high. In contrast, a bullish divergence occurs when the price makes a new low but the RSI makes a higher low. An RSI reversal on the other hand represents the opposite of divergence.

Figure 8.9. Sample RSI indicator for intraday price data (*Source:* finance.yahoo.com)

Other interpretations of the RSI indicator refer to the detection of uptrends and downtrends. In general, uptrends trade between RSI 40 and 80, while downtrends trade between RSI 60 and 20. Based on these thresholds, it is observed that a bearish divergence normally only occurs in an uptrend. This means that the detection of an RSI bearish divergence represents a signal of a positive momentum, while an RSI bullish divergence delineates the onset of a downtrend.

8-5-3.   Bollinger Bands

Bollinger Bands are a measure of volatility overlaid on the price chart. They consist of a middle band which represents a simple moving average of the price calculated based on a 20-day timeframe, and two upper and lower bands which are typically set at 2 standard deviations above and below the middle band, respectively. An example of Bollinger Bands is shown in Figure 8.10.

The gap separating the two outer bands widens when volatility increases, and narrows when it decreases. As such, Bollinger Bands are used to determine if prices are relatively high when the price chart crosses the upper band, or relatively low when the price chart crosses the lower band.

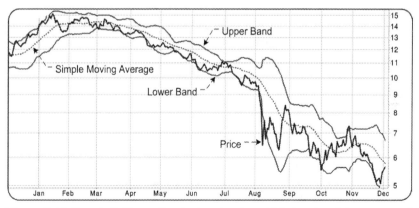

Figure 8.10. Sample Bollinger Bands showing the middle band and the upper and lower bands overlaid on a price chart (*Source:* www.stockcharts.com)

Two indicators are typically derived from the Bollinger Bands. The first one is known as the *percent-b* (%b) which defines the position of the current price relative to the two outer bands. This means that the value of %b is equal to zero (0%) when the price touches the lower band, and equal to 1 (100%) when the price touches the upper band. Such extreme values infer an oversold (0%) or overbought (100%) position of the security.

The second indicator derived from the Bollinger Bands is called the *Bandwidth*, which defines the volatility rate by measuring the size of the gap that separates the upper band from the lower band. The bandwidth thus increases when price volatility becomes more significant, or otherwise decreases when volatility lessens.

From a trading perspective, the interpretation of the Bollinger Bands varies considerably among traders. For instance, some traders formulate a buying position when the price touches the lower band (%b = 0), and a selling position when the price breaks through the middle band. Others prefer to sell their position when the price touches the upper band (%b = 1).

In either case however, the soundness of the formulated position should be strengthened by combining the analysis of the Bollinger Bands with the interpretation of other chart patterns and market indicators, as is typically the case when trading stocks based on technical data analysis.

Chapter 9

SMART SOFTWARE

9-1.   WHAT IS SMART?

SMART is an *experimental* software interface designed to retrieve intraday market data and create free financial databases for selected stocks trading on the floors of NYSE, NASDAQ and AMEX.

SMART's acronym stands for ***S**tock-data for **M**arket **A**nalysis and **R**esearch **T**ools*, and its computational engine is optimized to communicate with the Internet and retrieve market data at the end of every trading session. The retrieved data is stored inside a database that SMART creates and indexes automatically on the host computer. This database is routinely updated by SMART anytime a new data collection session is initiated.

The preliminary features and modes of operation of SMART are demonstrated through narrated tutorials available on *YouTube* Channel: www.youtube.com/user/STOCKTRADINGBOOK.

9-2.   MOTIVATIONS OF SMART

Discrete-time market data is not freely accessible to individual market researchers and technical analysts. Although open-access web pages such as *Yahoo!* offer free visual access to market data in the form of quotes and charts, the discrete-time numbers that constitute this data cannot be freely downloaded or accessed by personal financial software tools such as Excel or MATLAB.

This is because discrete-time market data, which represents the fundamental element of market models and quantitative analysis, is typically sold to research firms and academic business institutions for a price tag of about $10,000 per quarterly subscription.

This price tag is affordable for several business schools in the United States. However, for many smaller firms and individual research initiatives, the cost of this data is prohibitive, which effectively limits market research to affluent academic institutes and members affiliated with them. This implies that any prospective individual initiative of market modeling, no matter how promising it may be, cannot be tested and validated on factual data due to the prohibitive cost associated with accessing such information.

Based on these facts, SMART software was developed with the purpose of appealing to individual market researchers, by providing them with a tool that enables free access to discrete-time market data at the end of every trading session. Through SMART, market researchers can create their own databases of financial data that is compatible with existing mathematical and statistical software. This compatibility facilitates the validation of prospective market models using free real-time financial data.

Although SMART currently only exists at an experimental stage, its applicability to market research is a promising initiative for continual development, especially with regards to its ability to broaden market modeling to encompass any individual researcher with interest in financial statistics and technical analysis.

9-3.   MODES OF OPERATION

Retrieving data through SMART requires only a direct connection to the Internet. At the end of every trading session, discrete-time intraday public data for all stocks trading on the floors of NYSE, NASDAQ and AMEX are made available on the web, and thus can be accessed through SMART's fast computational engine.

This data remains available until the pre-market hours of the following trading session. However, with the *Auto* mode of SMART, the software can be configured to automatically communicate with the Internet at the end of every trading session, and retrieve market data for either a recurrent selection of stocks, or for the best performers of the day before such data is overwritten in the next trading session.

This can also be accomplished with SMART's second mode of operation which is the *Manual* mode. In this mode, the operator manually configures the interface to retrieve discrete-time market data for either the Top Gainers of the day, or for a selected number of customary symbols, or both.

A screen view of the experimental interface of SMART is provided in Figure 9.1, where the software is configured in the *Manual* Mode to retrieve market data for a list of thirteen stocks under the *Customary Symbols* option. This figure further shows the *Auto* Mode of SMART, as well as the tools that correspond to the two data retrieval options (Best Performers of the Day and Customary Symbols), and the common features to both.

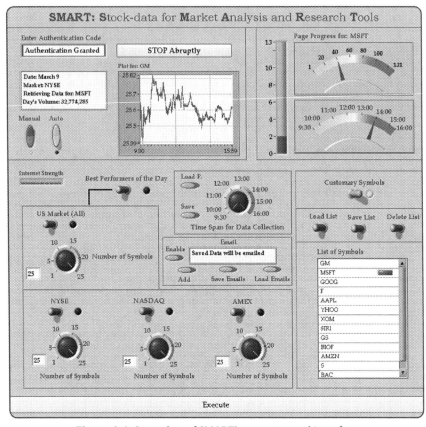

Figure 9.1. Snap-shot of SMART's experimental interface

9-3-1. Best Performers of the Day

SMART can be configured to retrieve discrete-time market data for the best performers of the day. This can be accomplished for the top gaining stocks across the entire US stock market, or for the top gaining stocks of individual markets (NYSE, and/or NASDAQ and/or AMEX).

Up to twenty-five top gaining stocks can be retrieved from every market at the end of every trading session. Once configured in this mode, SMART communicates with the web to locate the specified number of stocks, and retrieve their respective intraday discrete-time price/volume data and quotes. This data is then saved inside the financial database that SMART creates and indexes automatically on the host computer.

9-3-2. Customary Symbols

SMART can also be configured to retrieve discrete-time market data based on pre-selected stock symbols. In this mode, a list of customary stocks can be compiled, updated, or saved and reloaded for recurrent subsequent use. The selected stocks can be associated with any trading floor in the United States.

Once a list is compiled, SMART communicates with the web to sort out the symbols based on their markets (NYSE, NASDAQ, AMEX) before retrieving their respective discrete-time intraday data. The retrieved data, along with the day quote, are saved in the indexed database on the host computer.

9-3-3. Timeframes

The timeframe of the intraday data retrieved by SMART can also be defined by the operator. For instance, an operator might choose to retrieve market data for either the entire intraday session, or for a selected period of the intraday session.

This can be accomplished by defining the start and end times of the data collection process. For example, some researchers may be interested in the high trading activities exhibited at the opening of every trading session, and thus might choose to restrict the data retrieval process to a timeframe between 9:30 AM and 11:00 AM.

The default timeframe is the one that defines the duration of the entire session. However, if a custom frame is selected, it can be saved for the

Auto mode or for future recurrent use. SMART automatically limits the data collection process to the time interval specified by the operator via this option.

9-4.   INTERFACE DISPLAYS

SMART communicates the retrieved intraday data and the progress of the data collection process using multiple displays. For a sequence of selected stock symbols, SMART displays price information on a time-chart (Figure 9.1) as soon as the data is collected for every symbol in the sequence.

The progress of the data retrieval process is also visualized for each stock using two meters (Figure 9.1). The top meter displays the progress relative to the number of web pages that SMART has to open in the background. The second meter shows the progress towards the end of the pre-defined timeframe. For example, if an operator defines a timeframe of 9:30 to 11:00 AM, SMART will automatically adjust the upper bound of the second meter to 11:00 AM.

SMART also visualizes the progress towards the completion of the assigned task. This is done via a *fill-tank* display which fills by an extra notch every time the data for a featured symbol in the task is retrieved. The height of this display is automatically adjusted by SMART based on the total number of stocks selected for the assigned task.

9-5.   DATA INDEXING

The market data that SMART retrieves for every stock is split into two components. The first component depicts the day quote of the stock, and occupies the top three rows of the spreadsheet where the data is saved. The second component is a three-column matrix which contains the intraday price and volume data for the stock. The first column in this matrix represents the time progression from the minimum bound towards the maximum bound of the selected timeframe. The second column is the price, and the third column is the volume at each time stamp.

A sample of such data file is visualized in Table 9.1. The elements of the top three rows carry the following meanings: A_1 and B_1 are the day's high and low prices ($), C_1 is the day's volume (shares), A_2 is the average volume (shares), B_2 is the previous closing price ($), C_2 and A_3 are the 52-Week high and low ($), B_3 is the market cap ($) and C_3 is a dummy element that completes the third row and is always set to zero.

The three columns that follow the top three rows are also shown in Table 9.1. The length of these columns depends on the stock's activity and selected timeframe. For stocks that trade on a heavy volume, the length of these three columns will be sizable.

These data-files are saved in a spread sheet format that is compatible with existing financial software. Such files are further indexed by SMART based on the market, the date of the trading session, and the symbol of the stock which is assigned to the name of the file.

SMART also offers the option of automatically emailing the entire data retrieved at the end of every assigned task. This data is zipped and appended as an attachment to an email that SMART generates and sends to a selected list of recipients once the task is complete.

Table 9.1. A sample data file showing the day quote in the top three rows, and the intraday price and volume data in the subsequent columns

A_1=3.13	B_1=2.44	C_1=1237411
A_2=621884	B_2=2.72	C_2=3.96
A_3=1.04	B_3=73497600	C_3=0

Time	Price	Volume
9:30:00	2.71	47945
9:30:01	2.71	21445
9:30:23	2.72	2100
9:31:58	2.70	1800
9:36:04	2.664	1000

9-6.   EXAMPLES

Two sample examples of intrday price data are shown in Figure 9.2. These examples consist of two stocks, one trading under $10, and the other trading above $10. A comparison between the actual and retrieved data is also provided for convenience.

The retrieved data is plotted using MATLAB. Based on this visualization, it is obvious that some minor differences exist between the two charts due to the two different filtering techniques applied to both the actual, and the retrieved data.

In fact, the retrieved data is more detailed than the actual data since SMART recovers all values correpsonding to the intraday price chart before any filtering is applied to such chart. Nonetheless, one should note that plotting the entire price data without applying any filtering makes the resulting chart extremely noisy.

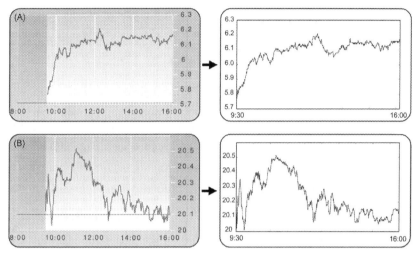

Figure 9.2. Two sample price charts showing the actual data (Left) and the retrieved data plotted on MATLAB (Right): (A) Sample stock trading under $10, (B) Sample stock trading above $10

Once the retrieved data is loaded and filtered on MATLAB (or any other similar financial software), it becomes easily accessible to test and validate the reliability of any prospective mathematical model. The day quote of each stock can also be loaded in a similar fashion for the same purpose.

9-7.   EXTENDED OPTIONS AND CONCLUSION

The basic features of SMART discussed in this chapter can be extrapolated to include many additional options. For instance, SMART can be limited to collecting quote data only (the first three rows in Table 9.1), without retrieving the intraday price and volume data. In such case, the speed of execution of these tasks will be significantly higher since SMART would have to open less web pages in the background.

In general, since quote data (open/close price and total volume) is mainly employed in technical analysis, limiting the scope of the data retrieval process allows SMART to extend the efficiency of its computational engine. This enables it to automatically retrieve and index quote data for all publically traded stocks in the United States at the end of every trading session.

SMART's options can be further extended to retrieve, and automatically update historical price and volume data for all stocks trading on the floors of NYSE, NASDAQ, and AMEX. This data includes open and close price, day's high and low, and daily volume for up to ten years of trading history.

These extended features, along with the ones discussed in this chapter, make SMART a potentially valuable tool that researchers can employ to access free market information, and create personal databases of financial data that constitutes the foundation of technical analysis and market modeling.

EPILOGUE

The expansion of Internet stock trading in the United States and around the globe is projected to continue as more small investors realize the opportunities for profit made available from the comfort of their personal computer. However, scouting the market for these opportunities on daily basis is a tricky process. This is due to the risk associated with stock trading, where individual investors can inflict significant losses to their online accounts if their trading positions are not formulated based on a fundamental understanding of the forces that drive the market.

Internet Stock Trading and Market Research for the Small Investor presented a fresh perspective on online stock trading that synthesized three years of market research, analysis, and active trading. The short-term strategies recommended in this book simplify the trading dynamics for small investors down to a fundamental interpretation of corporate news on daily basis. This eliminates the prerequisite of technical charting and analysis, and enables first-time traders to formulate sensible positions that minimize risk exposure by excluding the speculative component from the trading strategies.

The content of this book offered an encompassing introduction to market dynamics and regulations. It also presented a detailed, figure-supported discussion on news interpretation and free online resources that small investors can adopt to access market information based on which trading positions are formulated.

In short, *Internet Stock Trading and Market Research for the Small Investor* recommends the formulation of trading positions based on the interpretation of the Top Gainers List. In general, stock symbols featured on this list show the most potential for short-term price increase on daily basis.

An interpretation of the corporate news driving this short-term interest enables investors to identify the symbols with the strongest and most factually supported momentum. Such momentum typically represents an unusual-volume reaction to the release of corporate news that carries market connotations. Once these stocks are identified, an analysis of their quotes and extended price charts follows in order to evaluate potential signs of undervaluation. If such signs are present, a short-term buying position formulated at the beginning of the intraday trading session typically generates profits to an extent that depends upon the significance of the market connotations.

Selling these positions should be based on the significance of corporate news, as well as the interpretation of intraday price charts for signs of saturation. Many recurrent and reliable trends were discussed in this book to assist investors in detecting these saturation levels. Selling short-term positions is thus recommended at the onset, or at the end of a saturation zone prior to the attenuation of the short-term momentum.

The second part of this book carried a more technical component which targets individual market researchers. The aim of this part was to discuss a new experimental financial software interface called SMART (*Stock-data for Market Analysis and Research Tools*).

SMART enables free access to discrete-time market data that represents a fundamental component for financial modeling and quantitative analysis. Such data is typically sold as quarterly subscriptions for a price tag that is largely unaffordable by individual researchers. With SMART however, access to this data is free, which enables independent market researchers to create their own personal databases of financial data that can be employed for the validation of any prospective market modeling initiative.

Because SMART is currently at an experimental stage, access to the software is not yet available. However, an initial insight into SMART's interface can be acquired through the narrated tutorials available on *YouTube* Channel: www.youtube.com/user/STOCKTRADINGBOOK.

This simplified combination of the trading and research aspects of the stock market—separated into two independent parts—leaves the reader with a fundamental understanding of the market dynamics, and the sensible buying and selling strategies that maximize profit in the current environment of economic volatility.

RECOMMENDED READINGS

Toni Turner, "A Beginner's Guide to Day Trading Online," *Adams Media*, 2nd Edition, January 2007.

Matt Krantz, "Investing Online for Dummies," *For Dummies*, 7th Edition, August 2010.

Peter Schiff and Andrew Schiff, "How an Economy Grows and Why It Crashes," *Wiley*, 1st Edition, May 2010.

Jason Kelly, "The Neatest Little Guide to Stock Market Investing," *Plume*, Revised Edition, December 2009.

Kathy Kristof, "Investing 101," Bloomberg Press, 2nd Edition, August 2008.

Michael Sincere, "Start Day Trading Now: A Quick and Easy Introduction to Making Money while Managing your Risk," *Adams Media*, 1st Edition, March 2011.

Michael Thormsett, "Getting Started in Stock Investing and Trading," *Wiley*, Original Edition, December 2010.

Peter Leeds, "Invest in Penny Stocks: A Guide to Profitable Trading," *Wiley*, Har/Dol Edition, February 2011.

Jacob Bernstein, "The Ultimate Day Trader: How to Achieve Consistent Day Trading Profits in Stocks, Forex, and Commodities," *Adams Media*, 1st Edition, August 2009.

Ian Wyatt, "The Small-Cap Investor: Secrets to Winning Big with Small-Cap Stocks," *Wiley*, 1st Edition, August 2009.

Richard Imperiale, "The Micro Cap Investor: Strategies for Making Big Returns in Small Companies," *Wiley*, 1st Edition, January 2005.

Marcus Heitkoetter, "The Complete Guide to Day Trading: A Practical Manual from a Professional Day Trading Coach," *Outskirts Press*, 1st Edition, June 2008.

Van Tharp, "Trade Your Way to Financial Freedom," *McGraw-Hill*, 2nd Edition, November 2006.

Greg Capra, "Intra-Day Trading Tactics: Pristine.Com's Strategies for Seizing Short-Term Opportunities," *Marketplace Books*, Pap/DVD Edition, September 2007.

Michelle Hooper, "Online Investing: Everything You Need to Know Explained Simply," *Atlantic Publishing Group Inc.*, 1st Edition, January 2008.

GLOSSARY

52-Week price range—The highest and lowest price a stock reaches in one year of trading.

Acquisition—A corporate action where a large firm purchases the assets of a smaller firm and annexes them to its business portfolio.

All or none (AON)—A condition imposed on brokers instructing them to execute orders only if all shares are either bought or sold at once.

Ask price—The minimum price a seller of a stock is willing to accept for selling a share of that stock.

Ask size—The number of shares a seller is willing to sell at the ask price.

Average volume—Daily trading volume calculated as the total intraday share volume averaged over a period of three months or a full year.

Bear market—A down-trend in the indices over a period of time reflecting investors' loss of confidence in the market.

Bid price—The maximum price a buyer of a stock is willing to pay for a share of a given stock.

Bid size—The number of shares a buyer is willing to purchase at the bid price.

Bollinger Bands—A technical indicator that determines the highness or lowness of the current stock price relative to the moving average of pervious trades.

Bull market—An uptrend in the indices reflecting the increase in confidence and investors' optimism in the market's prospects.

Buying to cover—The process of buying the original number of shares in order to close an open position resulting from a short sell.

Candlestick—A charting technique that visualizes a progression of open and close prices for a chosen time period, along with the high and low bounds of the price during every trading session in the sequence.

Chart—A visualization technique that reflects the history of a stock price and volume data over a period of time which could span one day, or could extend to as far back as the initial public offering of the stock.

Commission—A fee investors pay to their brokers for executing a trade transaction resulting from a buying or a selling order.

Delisting—The practice of removing the stocks of a company from the stock exchange in the event of bankruptcy filing or failure to satisfy listing requirements.

Earnings per share (EPS)—Total quarterly profit or loss of a company, divided by the common outstanding shares. The EPS value may be positive (profit) or negative (loss).

Earnings report—A quarterly filing by public companies that reports the results of operations in the previous quarter, including revenues, cost of operation, profits, losses, EPS, *etc.*

Free ride—A violation of trade regulations which occurs with cash accounts when the unsettled proceeds of a selling order are used to place a new buying order which is subsequently sold prior to the settlement time.

Index—A statistical metric that measures the performance of the market as a whole, or the performance of specific sectors of the market on daily basis, and over the course of a period of time.

Initial public offering (IPO)—The event during which a company offers its common shares for public trading for the first time.

Insider trading—Trading activities initiated by individuals with access to non-public information about a company.

Intraday session—Trading session that starts at 9:30 AM (EST) and ends at 4:00 PM (EST) in the United States.

Kagi—A charting technique consisting of thin and thick vertical lines connected together by short horizontal lines with the objective of reducing random price noise.

Leverage—The practice of increasing an investor's purchasing capability by borrowing money against the account's assets which serve as the collateral for this line of credit.

Limit order—A trading action that defines the minimum price at which a specified number of shares should be sold, or the maximum price at which the requested shares should be bought.

Liquidity—The ease of buying into, or selling out of a stock.

Long trading—Traditional form of trading where profit is derived from appreciation of the security (stock) over time.

Margin trading—The practice of trading securities (stocks) by borrowing money against the account's asset value which defines the collateral for this type of transactions.

Market capitalization—The monetary value of a company's total public assets, calculated by multiplying the share price of the company's public stock offering by the number of issued shares.

Market order—A buy or sell order executed at the best price available, without specifying such price.

Merger—A corporate action where two companies consent on combining assets to create a new larger firm.

Moving average—Statistical filters that smooth out the noisiness of a price chart.

Penny stock—A stock with a share price of under $1.

Price change—A percentile comparison between the price of a share during any given trading session, and the closing price of the previous session.

Quote—A list of metrics that characterizes the movement of a stock during regular market hours, and summarizes relevant statistical measures about the stock performance over the course of a selected period of time.

Renko—A charting technique consisting of a diagonal sequential cascade of hollow and filled bricks plotted against a selected time period, where the spacing along the time-axis is not uniform.

Resistance—The price level at which the stock experiences more selling than buying activities, causing the share price to reach a saturation level beyond which the stock cannot maintain its positive momentum.

Reverse split—A corporate action that increases the share price and decreases the number of common shares in a company without affecting its market capitalization.

SEC (Securities and Exchange Commission)—The federal agency that enforces federal laws and regulates stock trading activities in the United States.

Settlement time—The three-day period at the end of which a broker must pay for the stocks sold by an investor.

Share price—The amount of money a buyer pays to acquire a single share in a public company's common stock offering.

Share Volume—The sum of the total number of shares bought or sold during a given period of time, or over the course of one trading session.

Short trading—A trading strategy where investors generate profit by bidding on the fact that a given security (stock) will lose value during the time they are holding it.

Split (stock)—A corporate action that decreases the share price and increases the number of common shares in a company without affecting its market capitalization.

Spread—The difference between the ask price and the bid price.

Stock exchange—The floor where most trading and brokerage activities take place. A stock exchange is also the entity that regulates and controls the exchange and pricing of equities (stocks) between buyers and sellers.

Stop order—A trading position triggered with a buy action when the stock price exceeds the stop price, or with a sell action when the stock price falls below the stop price.

Stride (price)—The price gain that a stock achieves between one support level and the following resistance or support level.

Support—The price level at which the stock experiences more buying than selling activities, preventing the share price from dropping any further as the stock is losing value.

Symbol (Stock)—A combination of one, two, three, or four letters (rarely numbers) that uniquely abbreviate the name of a public company trading on a stock exchange floor.

Technical analysis—The practice of forecasting the future movement of a stock based on past and current price and volume information.

Top gainers list—A statistical table that sorts in a descending order, up to twenty-five stocks based on the percentage increase in share value during every trading session.

Top losers list—A statistical ranking scheme that features stocks whose share value drops the most during every trading session.

Top most active list—A statistical ranking scheme that sorts stocks based on share volume, irrespective of the price percent change.

Volatility—A measure of the speed or amplitude of variations of a stock price over time.

Volume—The sum of the total number of shares bought or sold over the course of one trading session.

INDEX

A

Acquisition 96, 97
After-hours 9, 10, 20, 21, 68, 69
All or none (AON) 42, 43
AMEX 3, 4, 8, 55
Ask price 18, 19
Ask size 18, 19
Average volume 14, 15, 82 161

B

Bandwidth 154
Bear market 26, 41, 42
Bid price 18, 19
Bid size 18, 19
Blue chip 60
Bollinger Bands 153, 154
Bull market 26
Buying to cover 41, 42

C

Cash account 38, 39, 47-49, 51, 52
Candlestick chart 135, 136
Chart pattern 140
Close price 15, 18, 21, 59, 61, 63, 135, 161
Commission 31-33, 43, 44

D

Delisting 4, 30, 97, 101

Discount brokers 32

Dow Jones 5-7

E

Early trading hours 9, 10, 20, 21

Earnings Per Share (EPS) 24, 93

Earnings report 24, 25, 92-96

Extended charts 63-65

F

Freeriding (Free ride) 33, 38, 48-52

Frozen account 52

I

Index (stock) 5-7

Initial Public Offering 29

Insider trading 28, 54, 133, 134

Interest rate 39, 40, 149

Intraday charts 63-65, 135

K

Kagi chart 137, 138

L

Lagging indicator 149

Leading indicator 149

Leverage 39, 40

Limit order 44

Limit price 44, 45, 47

Line chart 135

Liquidity 13, 14, 34, 58

Listing 3, 4, 30
Long (trading) 40-42

M
Maintenance fee 3, 37
Margin account 39, 40, 47, 48
Market capitalization 3, 4, 17, 29, 30
Market connotations 72-74
Market order 43-46, 51
Merger 96-98
Moving average 150, 151, 153

N
NASDAQ 3-5, 8
NASDAQ Composite 6, 7
News (corporate) 36, 70, 71
NYSE 3-5, 8
NYSE Composite 6, 7

O
One-year target estimate 20
Online brokerage firm 31, 33, 36
Open price 15, 16
Order execution speed 33, 34
OTC 4, 5, 9, 20, 55
Overlays 23, 148, 150
Overvaluation 16, 23, 134

P
Penny stock 27, 28, 30, 32, 44
Percent-b (%b) 153, 154
Pink sheets 4, 5, 9 20, 55
Pre-market 9, 10, 20, 68, 69, 118

Price chart 13, 16, 22, 23
Price range (52-Week) 15-17
Price percent change 18, 55, 57, 58

Q
Quote 10, 11, 20, 21, 30, 36, 60-62, 68, 69, 71

R
Regular market hours 9, 10, 20, 21, 68, 69
Regulation T 47-49, 52
Renko chart 138-140
Resistance 26, 27, 67, 116, 117, 120, 122, 123, 137
Reverse stock split 29, 30

S
Saturation zone 119-122, 166
Securities and Exchange Commission (SEC) 3, 24
Settled funds 48, 49, 51, 52
Settlement time 38, 47-49
Share price 12, 14-16, 18, 29, 30, 34, 60, 62, 63, 67
Short (trading) 40-42
SMART 155, 156, 158
Split (stock) 29, 30
Spread 19
Stair-like ascending chart 116, 117
Stock exchange 3, 4, 8
Stop limit order 45
Stop order 45, 46
Stop price 40, 45, 46
Stride (Price) 122-124, 145
Symbol (Stock) 8, 9, 57, 58

T

Technical analysis 131-133, 156

Technical indicator 132, 149-154

Ticker 8

Top gainers list 54-57, 59, 68

Top losers list 59, 60

Top most active list 59, 60

Trade regulations 47

Trailing stop limit order 45, 46

Trailing stop order 45, 46

Trend line 141, 147

U

Undervaluation 16, 23, 28, 76, 80, 87, 93, 98, 100, 113, 125

Unsettled funds 49, 50, 52

Update frequency 32, 34-36, 54, 56, 61, 65, 70

V

Volatility 13, 19, 27, 33, 43, 51, 153, 154

Volume (share) 12, 20, 21, 63

Volume chart 21, 22, 64, 66, 69